an Indigo
CELEBRATION

Also by Lee Carroll and Jan Tober

The Indigo Children
The New Kids Have Arrived

(also available in Spanish, Hebrew, Dutch,
Russian, French, Hungarian, German, and Japanese)

Other Hay House Titles of Related Interest

The Body Knows
How to Tune In to Your Body and Improve Your Health,
by Caroline M. Sutherland, Medical Intuitive

The Care and Feeding of Indigo Children,
by Doreen Virtue, Ph.D.
(Foreword by Jan Tober)

The Power of Touch
The Basis for Survival, Health, Intimacy, and Emotional Well-Being,
by Phyllis K. Davis, Ph.D.

Power Thoughts for Teens, *a 50-Card Deck,*
by Louise L. Hay

Practical Parenting,
by Montel Williams and Jeffrey Gardère, Ph.D.

What Color Is Your Personality?
Red, Orange, Yellow, Green . . . ,
by Carol Ritberger, Ph.D.

All of the above are available at your local bookstore,
or may be ordered through Hay House, Inc.:

(800) 654-5126 or (760) 431-7695
(800) 650-5115 (fax) or (760) 431-6948 (fax)
www.hayhouse.com

an Indigo
CELEBRATION

More Messages, Stories, and Insights
from the Indigo Children

Lee Carroll
and
Jan Tober

Hay House, Inc.
Carlsbad, California • Sydney, Australia

Copyright © 2001 by Lee Carroll and Jan Tober

Published and distributed in the United States by: Hay House, Inc., P.O. Box 5100, Carlsbad, CA 92018-5100 • (800) 654-5126 • (800) 650-5115 (fax) www.hayhouse.com

Editorial supervision: Jill Kramer • *Design:* Charles McStravick

Library of Congress Cataloging-in-Publication Data

Carroll, Lee.
      An indigo celebration / Lee Carroll and Jan Tober.
            p. cm.
      Includes bibliographical references.
      ISBN 1-56170-859-3 (tradepaper)
            1. Children--Psychic ability--Case studies. 2. Human evolution--
Miscellanea. I. Tober, Jan (Jan M.) II. Title.

BF1045.C45 C37 2001
133.8'083—dc21

2001026411

ISBN 1-56170-859-3

04 03 02 01   4 3 2 1
1st printing, October 2001

Printed in Canada

❧ Contents ❧

◈ Acknowledgments ◈

Some of the people who made this book possible:
(in order of appearance)

Nancy Coleman
William Linville
Kim Mander
Mallika Krishnamurthy
Steve Arnold
Cher Matthews
Allison Hurley
Connie Mann
Marie-Helene Dubois
Petra-Sarah Neumayer
Dee
Gousei Robert Jacobs
Grace Kohl
Nancy Shea
Sharon Marshall
Jere Neal
Marcia Pack
Doris Crompton
Justine Turner
Jenny Marrs
Kathryn Hutson
Brian Coleman
Joanne Wisor
Monique E. LeBlanc
Constance Snow
Gabby van Heerden
Renee Weddle
Anne Saunders
Susan Saunders
Jennifer Walsh
Robin Rowney
Sally Donovan

Bev Wells
Katherine
Barbra Dillenger
Nikki Dolan
Felicitas Baguley
Evelyn Beatty
Tracy Cisneros
Yvonne Zollikofer
Kerry-Lynne Findlay-Chapman
Angela Graves
Anna
Bea Wragee
Mary Ann Gildroy
Rabbi Wayne Dosick
Nan Sunshine
Umar Sharif
Jaye Powers
Barbara Brandt
Mike Meloy
Joyce Tutty
Vanessa
Pamela Hollander
Nancy Tappe
Sharyl Jackson
Barbara Gilman
Shirley Michaels
Lisa Wallace
Katarina Friedrich
Patty Doe
Jacob Butler
Betsie Poinsett
Karen Eck (thank you!)

"Children are our greatest untapped resource."
— The Dalai Lama[1]

"Each child is an adventure into a better life—
an opportunity to change the old pattern
and make it new."
— Hubert H. Humphrey[1]

"If help and salvation are to come, they can only come from
the children, for the children are the makers of men."

— Maria Montessori, Italian educator[1]

Introduction

This is the second Indigo Children book we've published, but it really isn't a sequel to the last one. In other words, we're changing gears at bit and are going to present some information from the parents along with some more profound wisdom from teachers and professionals. Whereas the first book was an explanation and revelation of the Indigo subject, this book is less intensely academic, and more fun. That means: *Expect some humor.*

Jan and I would like to believe that everyone who picks up this book has read the original Indigo Child book called *The Indigo Children*, published in 1999 by the same company that's putting out this one (Hay House).

We can't assume that, however, so if you're reading this book and are asking, "What's an Indigo Child?" we will briefly synopsize the message of the original best-selling Indigo book.

A review: Jan and I are self-help lecturers and authors. When you're counselors and you spend a lot of time with people dealing with humanistic attributes, there are often patterns of behavior that emerge that aren't necessarily obvious to those who don't see "the big picture."

As we said in the last book, we started hearing more and more about a new kind of child—or at least a new kind of problem for the parent. The difficulties were odd in nature, in that they represented an interchange between adult and child that was unexpected and seemingly atypical of what our generation (or even the one after ours) had experienced.

Many parents were exasperated and at their wit's end. Day-care workers all over the nation, some of whom had worked in their profession for more than 30 years, were also telling us the same kind of stories—about how things were somehow different with these kids.

We realized that this wasn't limited to American children, since in our world travels we had spoken to many parents with identical issues. Even the Asian culture, which seemed in the past to produce children who grew up to honor and respect their parents through cultural training, was beginning to exhibit the same behavioral anomalies (see Chapter 8).

So we wrote *The Indigo Children* and had tremendous help from highly respected authors, academic contributors, day-care workers, Ph.D.'s, M.D.'s, and others who work with children on a daily basis

We stepped out on a limb, offering the best information we could about what we observed on a subject that we knew might be controversial. After all, who were we to tap society on the shoulder and say, "Excuse us, but we think that humankind is evolving, and the kids are the proof"?

Well, we were right—the subject was indeed controversial, and we received a combination of hate mail and a plethora of thanks for saving children's lives—all in the same mailbag! What do you do with that? The answer is simple: Throw away the ones you don't like and only print the nice ones on your Web page!

Seriously, though, the one factor that gave us confidence was that the book was so well accepted. It was distributed around the world within months, was translated into many foreign languages, and outsold any book we'd ever written before. To us, this meant that people were truly relating to the message. Either that, or they were lining a bunch of bird-cages with the pages of our book.

Bookstores all over America started carrying *The Indigo Children,* and they realized that they had a marketing quandary (a positive one): where to put the book in the store? We found it on the shelves of Barnes & Noble under "Parenting," and then again under "New Age." Some also told us that certain stores put it into the Children's section. We thought that was odd, since we wrote the book for adults, not kids. We found out later that some children were demanding that the parents purchase the book and read it to them! Somehow they related to the subject just by hearing the title (we're getting weird now).

We also found the book in Costco, a discount ware-house store where you buy paper goods and drinks by the truckload—you know the kind. In some other states, it's a chain called Sam's. We didn't know if this was a compliment to the book or not, but now we've decided that it was a good thing. In our town, San Diego, the Indigo books are right by the 80-pound paper clip boxes. Now when folks go there, they pass our Indigo books on their way to buy toilet paper by the ton.

We eventually set up a Website: **www.indigochild.com,** which thousands of people visited within the first eight months of the book's release. Many professionals now carry the book in their offices, and some require it to be read as part of their work. We also knew of several school principals who obtained the books by the caseload and put one on the desk of every teacher in the school!

Indeed, the book sparked an amazing response in the last year, and Jan and I found ourselves giving interviews regarding the subject from the very controlled studios of Singapore Radio (in Singapore), to the coast-to-coast "anything goes" Dreamland radio show here in the States—formerly hosted by Art Bell, and now by Whitley Streiber. (We were on the latter show twice.) But where would we go from there?

Some accused us of being biased in our spiritual belief system (metaphysics), and of promoting a cult of kids (these were very angry letters). Our response was that we simply couldn't leave God out of this picture. If people were looking for an empirical study using kids as lab rats, they would be disappointed by our research. This was about life, and about profound situations developing all over the nation and around the world. Our spiritual "take" on the subject turned out to be one that also made it into some other books written about the same phenomenon (discussed below).

We were not subscribing to any church or religion, but rather, reporting on the *spiritual* aspects of certain Indigo behaviors. It turns out that many of these children are often interested in religion and their own spirituality. The church is their own choice (of course). So if the kids want to talk about God, we're going to let you know about it. Many of the kids see angels! Some parents think this is a problem and want to call Ghostbusters or run to the local exorcist (honest!), so we want to assure them that the kids are okay. In fact, we think they're *more* than okay.

If you want a hoot, go to **www.amazon.com** and read the reviews. They're either five-star or one-star. Those who hated it didn't understand what we were trying to point out. Some it didn't help at all, and some it helped greatly. Others actually concluded that we were promoting the fact that these new children on Earth were space aliens! We weren't, but we *were* telling people that we felt that this was a new kind of evolution of humanity. Regardless of the mixed reviews, after two years, *The Indigo Children* is often still in the top 600 on Amazon's list.

This is important: *We don't own the Indigo subject.* We only introduced and reported what we knew and what we saw. We were also aware that more information would follow as the phenomenon was recognized. We didn't know how quickly, however. At the same time we published *The Indigo Children,* two other mainstream books were released about the same subject: *Children of the New Millennium: Children's Near-Death Experiences and the Evolution of Humankind),* by P. M. H. Atwater[2;] and *Old Souls: The Scientific Evidence for Past Lives,* by Tom Shroder.[3] Both of the books were about Indigo Children; they just didn't *call* them Indigos. We wonder if they received angry religious letters, too—or whether people thought the kids in *their* books were from outer space.

We are still at the head of the pack in the mega-warehouse store, however. We don't see either of these other books next to ours when we go to buy napkins by the bushel, or the humongous jar of peanut butter that will last you five years. We kind of like that.

The Purpose of This Book

As we said earlier, this really isn't a sequel to our last book. There are many fine authors out there who are picking up the ball and providing the "how to's" with respect to parenting the Indigos. Here, we want to depart a bit from academia and make this a *celebration* of the Indigo experience. We want a soft read, a breath of fresh air, laughter, fun, and some tears. We also want to broach a couple of subjects that we didn't get to in the first book, such as those who feel they were Indigo Children but who are way too old to fit the age parameters we stated. We'll present some solid information, too—some of it very serious—about children killing children, what to do to help our teens, and the importance of Inner Child work for adults. But we do want to forewarn you that you may also have some fun along the way.

Many parents wrote us with their Indigo stories. They were heartwarming, enlightening, and even sad. But all of them were about life with the Indigos—an exceptional group of children growing up on Earth who are intelligent, savvy, and who don't respond at all like the children of previous generations. So the purpose of this work is to provide some amusement as well as some intellectual and educational stimulation. We want this book to give you insights into real experiences, and we also want it to entertain you with the things children have said and done, as reported by their parents.

So when appropriate, take off your academic hat and put on your party hat. Celebrations are fun, and we give you permission to laugh, cry, gasp, yell, and exclaim, "Hey, my kid does that, too!" Then, if you didn't read the first book, you might read it to see what this is all about. Go to your local "mega-store" and get a truckload of paper towels while you're at it. They're just up the aisle from the stack of Indigo books—right next to the one-year supply of raisin bran.

Organization

Okay . . . about organization. We'd like to yell the words, "THERE ISN'T ANY!" That's our Inner Kid speaking, wishing we didn't have to have chapters, endnotes, or any of that boring stuff (see Chapter 5 for more on the Inner Child). But we do. Not too much, though.

The first part of the book is a series of stories submitted by adults and some children. Some are very short; others are longer. We'll intersperse them with sayings by the children, and even some poetry.

As we mentioned, there's a short chapter honoring the older Indigos, and again (as in the last book), some letters from the Indigos themselves. We've also included a second interview with Nancy Tappe, our expert "color" lady, and some words of wisdom by a number of other contributors as well. We have a chapter on finding the Inner Child, which we believe is critical for good parenting, and finally, a wrap-up of what we've learned from educators, parents, the news, and society in general about parenting Indigos.

The Contributors

As far as the contributors are concerned, each time we introduce a story, we will try to give you the name of the contributing adult (or child in some cases). Some adults didn't want their real names given because they didn't want to embarrass their children when the kids grew up and read this book! Some children who wrote didn't want the real names of their parents given—kind of tells you about some relationships, doesn't it? So we've honored these specific requests. If you happen to find your story in here—one you wrote us in a letter a long time ago—and you've moved or changed your e-mail address in the meantime, it explains why your full name was not credited. In those cases, only first names have been used.

The Internet: The New Publishing Puzzle

We also encountered a dilemma that was somewhat new to us: how to give credit to unknown sources whose words originally appeared on the Internet. In publishing, you're supposed to have sources, or give credit to whatever is not your own writing. In the case of kids or parents who wrote things anonymously on the Web, we weren't quite sure what to do. We asked ourselves, do we simply ignore some great stuff (and very funny things), or publish them? There was an integrity issue involved.

So, here's what we chose to do: In this book, we *have* published the Internet jewels we found, and under the title, we've stated that the author is unknown and that the source was the Internet. If you read anything in this book that you feel is yours, or you recognize it as having been published and you know where it came from, please contact us right away at: **www.indigochild.com**. We can make necessary revisions to this book when it's reprinted, and we will definitely include any requested credits when appropriate. Simply write us and give us copyright information or some proof of ownership, and we will put the correct name with the reported quotations. In addition, we will publish the credit corrections on our Website so that they can be made public immediately. There is actually precedent for this in some other popular books, and we've decided to emulate what they've done.

We hope that this book brings you knowledge, insight, laughter, and hope for the future of our planet!

chapter one

The Wise Children

"What's the difference between an Indigo Child and Bart Simpson [of *The Simpsons* TV show fame]?" This amusing question was asked of Jan in an interview last year shortly after the first Indigo book was released. The answer? They both have an agenda, but each is very different. The bully (or Bart Simpson type) wants to get attention, and he will push and push and push to get it. After he gets what he wants, he will push some more to see what the limit is. The agenda of the Indigo Children is to push until they're understood, or at least included. Then they stop.

The wisdom of the Indigos is amazing to observe. They have some very profound life questions all figured out and ready to be served up to whoever listens. Even those who don't get it quite right are still showing wise thought processes.

We'd like to initiate this celebration with some sayings by children on love and relationships (a favorite topic to many of us):

Tips on Love
Unknown Author. Source: The Internet

When is it okay to kiss someone?

"You should never kiss a girl unless you have enough bucks to buy her a big ring and her own VCR, 'cause she'll want to have videos of the wedding." (Jim, 10)

Why does love occur between two particular people?

"No one is sure why it happens, but I heard it has something to do with how you smell. That's why perfume and deodorant are so popular." (Jan, 9)

What's it like to fall in love?

"It's like an avalanche where you have to run for your life." (Roger, 9)

"If falling in love is anything like learning how to spell, I don't want to do it. It takes too long." (Leo, 7)

What's the role of good looks in love?

"If you want to be loved by somebody who isn't already in your family, it doesn't hurt to be beautiful." (Jeanne, 8)

"It isn't always just how you look. Look at me, I'm handsome like anything, and I haven't gotten anybody to marry me yet." (Gary, 7)

"Beauty is skin deep. But how rich you are can last a long time." (Christine, 9)

Why do lovers often hold hands?

"They want to make sure their rings don't fall off because they paid good money for them." (Dave, 8)

What are your thoughts on love?

"I'm in favor of love as long as it doesn't happen when *The Simpsons* is on television." (Anita, 6)

"Love will find you even if you're trying to hide from it. I've been trying to hide from it since I was five, but the girls keep finding me." (Bobby, 8)

"I'm not rushing into being in love. I'm finding fourth grade hard enough." (Regina, 10)

What are the personal qualities necessary to be a good lover?

"One of you should know how to write a check. Because even if you have tons of love, there's still going to be a lot of bills." (Ava, 8)

What are some surefire ways to make a person fall in love with you?

"Don't do things like have smelly green sneakers. You might get attention, but attention ain't the same thing as love." (Alonzo, 9)

"One way is to take the girl out to eat. Make sure it's something she likes to eat. French fries usually work for me." (Bart, 9)

What are most people thinking when they say "I love you"?

"The person is thinking, *Yeah, I really do love him, but I hope he showers at least once a day.*" (Michelle, 9)

How can you make love last?

"Spend most of your time loving instead of going to work." (Tom, 7)

"Be a good kisser. It might make your wife forget that you never take out the trash." (Randy, 8)

Some of these sayings are not just funny—but also very astute! They make you wonder where all that wisdom came from. Here, a group of professionals posed the question, "What does love mean?" to a group of eight-year-olds. The answers they received were more profound than anyone could have imagined.

What Is Love?
Unknown Author. Source: The Internet

"Love is that first feeling you feel before all the bad stuff gets in the way."

"When my grandmother got arthritis, she couldn't bend over and paint her toenails anymore. So my grandfather does it for her all the time, even when his hands get arthritis, too. That's love."

"When someone loves you, the way they say your name is different. You know that your name is safe in their mouth."

"Love is when a girl puts on perfume and a boy puts on shaving cologne, and they go out and smell each other."

"Love is when you go out to eat and give somebody most of your French fries without making them give you any of theirs."

"Love is when someone hurts you. And you get so mad but you don't yell at them because you know it would hurt their feelings."

"Love is what makes you smile when you're tired."

"Love is when my mommy makes coffee for my daddy, and she takes a sip before giving it to him to make sure the taste is okay."

"Love is when you kiss all the time. Then when you get tired of kissing, you still want to be together and you talk more. My mommy and daddy are like that. They look gross when they kiss."

"Love is what's in the room with you at Christmas if you stop opening presents and listen."

"If you want to learn to love better, you should start with a friend who you hate."

"When you tell someone something bad about yourself and you're scared they won't love you anymore. But then you get surprised because not only do they still love you, they love you even more."

"There are two kinds of love: Our love. God's love. But God makes both kinds of them."

"Love is when you tell a guy you like his shirt, then he wears it every day."

"Love is like a little old woman and a little old man who are still friends even after they know each other so well."

"During my piano recital, I was on a stage and scared. I looked at all the people watching me and saw my daddy waving and smiling. He was the only one doing that. I wasn't scared anymore."

"My mommy loves me more than anybody. You don't see anyone else kissing me to sleep at night."

"Love is when Mommy gives Daddy the best piece of chicken."

"Love is when Mommy sees Daddy smelly and sweaty and still says he is handsomer than Robert Redford."

"Love is when your puppy licks your face even after you left him alone all day."

"I know my older sister loves me because she gives me all her old clothes and has to go out and buy new ones."

"I let my big sister pick on me because my mom says she only picks on me because she loves me. So I pick on my baby sister because I love her."

"Love cards like Valentine's cards say stuff on them that we'd like to say ourselves, but we wouldn't be caught dead saying."

"When you love somebody, your eyelashes go up and down and little stars come out of you."

"Love is when Mommy sees Daddy on the toilet and she doesn't think it's gross."

"You really shouldn't say 'I love you' unless you mean it. But if you mean it, you should say it a lot, because people forget."

There were so many stories we came across about the wisdom displayed by very young children that we often had a difficult time deciding which ones to eliminate—they were all great. For each story that you read here, there are about ten more that didn't make it to these pages. Today's children are not just wise—they're often our teachers! Here's a sample of what we mean.

Special Valentine
Nancy Coleman

Davis was four, and it was Valentine's Day at school. The children were required to give everyone in the class a Valentine. He said to me, "Mom, there's one kid who's really mean who doesn't deserve a Valentine. But I was thinking—maybe if I give him one and I treat him nice, even though he's not nice, that will help him feel better about himself." My heart swelled!

Zachary
William Linville

I'm pleased to share a few anecdotes regarding our seven-year-old son, Zachary. Zachary has made a significant difference in our lives. Thanks to him, my wife Laura and I have come to understand his purpose for us, and consequently, our own purpose has become clearer.

The story I wish to share happened when Zachary was six years old. One day I found him sitting in our living room on the sofa with his eyes closed. His toys were strewn about the room, and it was time for him to put them away. I said, "Zachary, it's time to pick up our toys, please." There was no response or acknowledgment from Zachary. Somewhat perturbed, I raised my voice and repeated my request, "Zachary, it's time to pick up our toys, please!!" To which he opened his eyes, looked me straight in the eyes, and said, "Not now, Dad, I'm talking with my Higher Self, and I'm not finished yet!"

Needless to say, I was beside myself upon hearing this unexpected response. Then I was overcome with great joy and understanding—so much so that we started to give him options and choices such as the ones you suggest in your book. Now, life flows much easier between us.

Zachary's first love is Mother Nature. The other day we were coming out of a health-food store and Zachary proceeded to describe why certain trees shed their bark and leaves and so on. I know Zachary hasn't covered this aspect of nature in his school curriculum, so out of curiosity, I asked him how he learned about trees. Zachary's reply was immediate and simple: "I just know, Dad."

My message to parents is to be aware of the possibilities that are inherent in today's children. Many children see through the facade of the "old ways of the world." They're here to bring us "home" and to show us a "better way," a more joyous and harmonious way of life. A way of life that helps us to experience our connectedness with all things and ALL THAT IS.

From a Three-Year-Old!
Kim Mander

I have a six-year-old boy who I think is an Indigo Child. However, he may not necessarily be an Indigo, but a spiritual being who is really "tuned in to" his gifts. He shares very profound insights and comments about matters that a normal six-year-old would not understand. One day we were driving down the road and I was very angry because he was really testing the boundaries and he made me late for my 8:00 A.M. meeting. I told him I was angry because of what he was doing, and out of the blue (this was when he was three years old), he said, "Mom, your conscience is the key." I asked him to explain, being shocked at what I had just heard, and he said, "It's that little voice inside your heart that tells you the right thing to do."

Just the other day, a little girl from next door was telling my son that her daddy could beat up his daddy because he was 46 years old and stronger. My son said, "It doesn't matter how strong you are on the outside. All that matters is how strong you are on the inside."

I have "journaled" his life since this comment, which was made at three years of age. He has said some pretty amazing things! He can see auras and often knows exactly what people are thinking. He has blondish-brown hair with big blue eyes, and he's very serious and often just observes instead of interfacing with people. His teachers say that he's beyond his years in knowledge for kindergarten, but he has trouble staying focused and doing work independently. My son says it's because the work is boring and stupid and because all you do is color.

Ready to hear more about relationships? How about marriage in general? Okay, here's another Internet offering on love, marriage, and gushy stuff like that. These are priceless gems!

Kids on Marriage
Unknown Author. Source: The Internet

How do you decide whom to marry?

"You've got to find somebody who likes the same stuff. Like, if you like sports, she should like it that you like sports, and she should keep the chips and dip coming." (Alan, age 10)

"No person really decides before they grow up who they're going to marry. God decides it all way before, and you get to find out later who you're stuck with." (Kirsten, age 10)

What is the right age to get married?

"Twenty-three is the best age because you know the person FOREVER by then." (Camille, age 10)

"No age is good to get married at. You've got to be a fool to get married." (Freddie, age 6)

How can a stranger tell if two people are married?
"You might have to guess, based on whether they seem to be yelling at the kids." (Derrick, age 8)

What do you think your Mom and Dad have in common?
"Neither wants any more kids." (Lori, age 8)

What do most people do on a date?
"Dates are for having fun, and people should use them to get to know each other. Even boys have something to say if you listen long enough." (Lynnette, age 8)

"On the first date, they just tell each other lies, and that usually gets them interested enough to go for a second date." (Martin, age 10)

What would you do on a first date that was turning sour?
"I'd run home and play dead. The next day I would call all the newspapers and make sure they wrote about me in all the dead columns." (Craig, age 9)

When is it okay to kiss someone?
"When they're rich." (Pam, age 7)

"The law says you have to be 18, so I wouldn't want to mess with that." (Curt, age 7)

"The rule goes like this: If you kiss someone, then you should marry them and have kids with them. It's the right thing to do." (Howard, age 8)

Is it better to be single or married?

"It's better for girls to be single, but not for boys. Boys need someone to clean up after them." (Anita, age 9)

How would the world be different if people didn't get married?

"There sure would be a lot of kids to explain, wouldn't there?"(Kelvin, age 8)

How would you make a marriage work?

"Tell your wife that she looks pretty even if she looks like a truck." (Ricky, age 10)

It seems to be starting very early, this wisdom thing. Yvonne Zollikofer speaks about Victor, her two-year-old. He asked one day, "Isn't it true, Mom, that I'm very old?" Her answer: "Yes, I think it is, my dear." I don't think Yvonne expected a question like that from a two-year-old mind.

Where does this early wisdom come from? Later we're going to broach the subject of kids speaking about spiritual (not religious) issues—some core concepts of life. But what about the Indigo attribute of self-worth? Are we really seeing it? Here's a short story—again about a human being who is barely old enough to know anything except the basics, yet who seems to know so much more.

Self-Worth
Mallika Krishnamurthy and Steven Arnold

Sashi, my six year old, has been showing quite a bit of wisdom, and a sense of knowing exactly who he is and what he is made of, all of his life. When he was two weeks old, the child health nurse commented that he seemed to have been here before.

When he was about two, we were at a large family gathering and he took himself to the car. We found him sitting quite peacefully in the dark, and we asked him what he was doing. He said he was just "thinking."

One day when he was perhaps three, we were talking about all the people he loved and who loved him. As we came to the end of a very, very long list, he said, "And I love myself because it gives me energy."

His life has been full of moments like that. He is full of wisdom and compassion and is an inspiration to us.

Sometimes the truth of what's *really* going on is shocking when it comes from children. Listen to Cher Matthews, a single mom, relate the observations of her three-year-old on her dating habits. It changed her ways!

The Envelope
Cher Matthews

My son Justin was born in 1980 and has exhibited the most classic Indigo behaviors his entire life. He was just "born knowing."

I've never forgotten something he said when he was three. It's written in his baby book, because I couldn't believe someone at the age of three could be so insightful!

I've always been a single mom. The men that I dated when my son was young would always try to "win my heart" by befriending Justin. Somehow Justin *knew* that these were not authentic attempts to really know *him*, but rather just a way of appeasing me.

To make a long story short, after one such date, my son commented to me, "You are the letter and I am the envelope." It was such a strange statement coming from someone so young! I asked him what he meant. He explained: "Everyone rips open the envelope to read the letter—and then they throw the envelope away." Needless to say, this broke my heart and still brings tears to my eyes. His perception changed my dating habits and created more awareness in me.

We've spoken in the past about how intuitive children are, even with respect to serious issues such as death and divorce. Here's a story about Ethan that will melt your heart. Children may not fully understand the "whys" of these things, but they definitely "feel" what's happening.

A Heart Rub
Allison Hurley

When my son was three years old, my husband and I got a divorce. For a variety of reasons, I had moved to England for a year and a half, and my ex-husband and I shared custody of Ethan.

From September to May, I made a few trips back to the U.S., but I did not really get to spend the time with Ethan that I wanted to. Finally, on Memorial Day, he came to live with me for the summer.

Before I could blink, summer was over and his dad flew in to pick him up. I was absolutely heartbroken. Ethan and I talked a lot about what was happening, and I was always amazed that he was so calm and centered about it all. He really seemed to comprehend what was happening.

At the airport, I got my final hugs and kisses before he boarded the plane with his dad. I tried to stay calm and focus on love, but I got very, very sad. Just before he boarded, he ran back to me and gave me a kiss on the cheek. He looked right into my soul, took his soft little hand and rubbed where he kissed, and said, "I'm rubbing it into your heart." And he was off.

Connie Man speaks of working with her 15-year-old, with her 9-year-old listening in the backseat. Perhaps you think the little ones don't always understand all that's going on? This might change your thinking.

Backseat Wisdom
Connie Man

My husband and I are blessed with three children: Melissa, 15; Joshua, 9; and Christiana, 3. My story involves Melissa and Joshua. One afternoon after picking up my two older children at school, Melissa began talking to me about the previous night. She and a few of her school friends had gone to a party, and Melissa wanted to know if I could explain an incident that had happened during the evening.

In order to clarify this situation, I will go back a few days when Melissa had asked for my assistance in helping her understand the dynamics of a certain relationship. Melissa and a boy at school, who really like each other, "pushed each other's buttons" quite often. She was aware that the way she felt in these encounters was a message and that this friend was playing the part of the messenger, so she wasn't asking how to change him, but rather how to "get" the message so that the dynamics of the relationship would change. I congratulated her on grasping this truth so early and suggested that we sit together and ask for guidance and clarity in this situation. We brought our awareness to our hearts, opened up to love, and Melissa stated her intent out loud. After a period of silence, we shared our thoughts and feelings, and Melissa decided that the next time she and this boy had a conflict, she would silently thank him for this opportunity, open her heart, and send him her love.

Back to the conversation in the car: Melissa shared that during the previous evening, this friend got angry with her and instead of yelling back, she silently thanked him, opened her heart, and sent him love. She said she could actually feel a sensation in her heart, and then a beam of light went from her heart to his, and for a few seconds all was quiet. Then, Melissa felt afraid and stopped the flow of love. She did not understand what had happened and was asking me to explain. I shared with her that opening your heart can make you feel very vulnerable and not to give up after the first try, as love is more powerful than fear.

My son, Joshua, was in the backseat playing with his little sister and not paying attention to our conversation—or so I thought. He leaned forward and said, "Missa, what if, when you opened your heart and were sending love to your friend, you felt his fear, not yours? What if his anger was fear?" I was nodding my head as feelings of awe and tears of joy and gratitude surged through me, making driving a bit difficult.

All I could say was, "Yes, yes, yes, Joshua! Of course that could be what happened. Melissa was transforming the fear with love."

Melissa and I continued to ponder his words of wisdom, and Joshua went back to playing with his little sister, not knowing that my heart was singing and my spirit was soaring, for I was blessed to be in the presence of these teachers of love—my children.

What does a child think about when he's ten months old? Can he grasp concepts such as helping Mom, or anything other than the subject of helping himself? The following is the classic Indigo situation. It might not seem like much, but consider what child-development experts tells you about these first months of life. An Indigo not only displays a "been there, done that" attitude, but also has some conceptual attributes that are way beyond what are expected. Here are some incidents that will make you stop and wonder about the differences between you and me at ten months old . . . and the new Indigos.

The Chair
Marie-Helène Dubois

When Ali was ten months old, he managed to push a chair into the kitchen. I was very angry, and I told him that the kitchen was too small to have a chair in it. I took the chair from him, and I put it back in the hall. Ali didn't cry and went to play elsewhere.

About three hours later, I saw that one of the three lightbulbs in the kitchen was burnt out, and I understood why Ali had pushed the chair into the kitchen. He just wanted to help me change the bulb, but he was too young to talk. I felt very guilty that day, and I promised myself to always try to see why my son was behaving in the way he was before getting angry at him. I didn't know about the Indigo children at that time, but I knew that my son was very special and somehow more intelligent than I.

You think that's unusual? Here's the same child at 14 months. Marie-Helène Dubois continues. . . .

When Ali was 14 months old, he opened the cupboard for the first time. My kitchen cupboard is very small, and I have a lot of pans of all sizes and all kinds. Everything is extremely well organized because the space is really limited and the two shelves are full. Ali came in, opened the cupboard, and started to take all the stuff out. I told myself, "Oh no! The kitchen will be a real mess, and I'll have to pick up everything!" But I left the room, leaving my son to have fun with his new game.

When I came back 20 minutes later, I had a big surprise. *Nothing* was on the floor! "Where are all my pans?" I wondered aloud. I opened the cupboard door and found that Ali had piled everything back in the exact place he had taken the pans from (and there were about 20 of them). Ali did the same thing *each time* he went to play with them.

Sometimes things seem to be almost beyond belief regarding these kids. Hey, if you're a mom, the last story must *really* seem unbelievable!

How about this one? We had many stories about children leading their parents into stores over the last year to find the first Indigo Children book! How would they know that it would help them (or their parents)? How would they know what it said? These are questions we can't answer, but here are two stories. The first is about David. It seems that he helped his parents find the book at a very appropriate time. The second one is about a boy who often reads with his mom—including the Indigo book!

On the Way to the Doctor
Petra-Sarah Neumayer

Thank you very much for your wonderful book, *The Indigo Children*. It saved my six-year-old son, David Nathan! This may seem exaggerated, but it's the truth. We were all ready to give up. Because our son is highly intelligent and extremely sensitive, he could not behave at all, or be with children his own age.

He started to talk when he was eight months old, and he learned to read and calculate by himself at the age of three. Now he's interested in science and astronomy. Each day he talks with God and with angels, whom he calls "my angels" and "my people." He says that he's a king, and he seems to know everything.

He was often very angry and aggressive with us because we didn't understand his behavior. We asked ourselves (and him) why he couldn't be "normal."

Finally, as I was on the way to a doctor who would have started to treat my son with Ritalin, David Nathan asked me to enter a certain store. He told me to look for the Indigo book. I had seen your book there, and I knew I had to buy it (I hadn't heard the expression "Indigo Children" before). From the moment I bought the book, my son's behavior changed. He seemed to be very happy and satisfied. And he still is!

P.S.: David will not be treated with Ritalin!

He Says I Did it Right
Dee

I just wanted to thank you for writing the Indigo book. I have a 13-year-old son who I believe is an Indigo Child. I often find myself telling others that he's different and you can't use traditional methods with him. I could never really explain what or why. Many of my family members swore that I had "lost" him a couple of years ago. I never lost faith in what he was and is to become, and I am now seeing a lot more of him "come alive." Your book has really helped me understand him better.

We had read about "The Indigo Children" in a news-paper article, and my son asked me to get the book and read it with him. He does have difficulty with reading and knew he would need help, but he has picked it up many times since I brought it home and read a few paragraphs. He tells me that I have instinctively done what the book suggests throughout his life.

I have also recommended the book to all my family members with children, and some of my son's teachers. I hope that it excites them as much as it did me!

What follows is a story that shows that some children look way beyond the violent movies and games of today, and actually have some insight about these things. Sometimes we don't think that children might be able to discern for themselves what is real or fantasy, so we restrict access to these types of games or shows. There is merit to doing so, but the following story reveals that some kids indeed understand the difference, even while experiencing it in reality.

Here is one boy who, in the midst of being actually trained in the martial arts, took an interesting stance. From the perspective of his karate teacher, here is the story of Jombi, the reluctant Indigo fighter.

The Training of Jombi
Robert Jacobs

I taught karate at a dojo in Florida during the '80s and '90s. During that time, I must have met a thousand kids. Most of the youngsters were memorable, some more than others; and one kid I'll never forget was a seven-year-old boy named Jombi. He was diagnosed with ADD (attention deficit disorder), and he was difficult to teach. We got the ADD-ers all the time. The parents brought the kids in hoping they'd learn to focus, or learn some self-discipline, or learn to learn. Jombi did a lot of staring and asked a lot of questions, but he was a nice, good-looking boy, and not much trouble. I was his teacher, or "Gousei," and I did my best with him.

I recall that whenever I taught him something, he wanted to know the "why" of it first, and then he would catch on more quickly. Sometimes we just didn't have time to explain things, so he wouldn't learn the technique.

One day I taught him to throw someone to the floor. I showed him how to step aside while grabbing his opponent's sleeve and lapel, then pivot while spinning the guy to the floor. He couldn't understand why we just didn't grab someone and throw him or her on the floor. I explained that some people were much larger, and one had to use cleverness to take them down. That appealed to Jombi, so he learned it.

He didn't understand why we repeated the kicks and punches, the aerobics portions of karate training. I explained that the repetition taught him to coordinate his body with his mind. He looked at me like I was crazy. I told him that once he did every kick and punch 1,000 times, he would be able to kick automatically without thinking about it. I got another blank stare. "Exercise is good for you," I said. "It will make you grow tall. Trust me." Jombi got with it.

He didn't want to kickbox. He couldn't see the sense in it. I told him that the kickboxing would strengthen and coordinate all his muscles at the same time, and he would learn to protect himself.

"Protect me from who?" he wanted to know.

"Well, maybe a bully in school," I answered.

"Why not just walk away?"

"We prefer to do that, but sometimes you can't; that's why we have karate schools."

"Why not just hit him?"

"I'm teaching you how to hit properly, Jombi."

"Why, Gousei Robert?"

"Because all those bad guys in the movies and the cartoons who lost the fights didn't know how to hit properly, and your mommy is paying for this, so toe the line, buddy, and put up your dukes."

He still didn't want to fight. He was afraid he would hurt someone. Argh! One of the little girls walked up, bonked him on top of the head, and said, "Come on, Jombi, this is fun!" Then he learned to kickbox, giggling away as he fought, but I let it go. Heck, I didn't want to discourage him. There's a science to fighting, and if Jombi wanted to giggle while learning the sweet science, so be it. I think I was more patient with Jombi than any other kid in that school—ever.

After he had been a student for about six months, it came time for Jombi to take his yellow belt test, the second rung up the ladder in my karate school. Jombi stood in the center of the dojo and showed that he had mastered all the kicks, blocks, and punches. He did the stylized forms, known as the *katas*. He performed the counterattacks to our satisfaction. He kickboxed a little girl, both of them giggling, while the owner of the studio, the master, admonished them to be serious. Jombi's mom and I just looked at each other.

Then it came time to break a couple of boards, and Jombi said he didn't want to do it. Oh, Lord, the very last thing on the test, and Jombi was having a meltdown. The master became impatient, and I was afraid he was going to dismiss Jombi. I said, "Let me talk to Jombi a second."

I put my head close to Jombi's and asked him why he didn't want to break the boards. He said the board was pretty and hadn't done anything to him. I asked him if he knew what tradition meant. He said, "Sort of. It was something you gave to someone else every year."

I said, "Close enough, Jombi. This is the scoop: All the karate skills you've learned have been passed down through the years from China, and we can directly trace our knowledge back 4,000 years. Jombi, all you have to do is break the boards and you'll be a part of ancient China. You've been taught the secret skills, and you'll be part of the tradition of the warrior priests. Do it for China, for yourself, and for your mom. Do it for me, Jombi. Just break the boards, please."

Jombi looked up and said, "China, huh?" I nodded.

Jombi broke the boards, his little war cries filling the dojo, and the master put the yellow belt on him. Jombi was no Bruce Lee, but he passed the test, and I was proud. I was proud of every kid in that school, but I felt something extra for Jombi; I thought he had a hard row to hoe. He soon left our little karate family, and his parents put him in another school district. He was too far away to attend classes with us. I saw him one more time when his mother brought him by. She wanted to buy another karate T-shirt for him. We talked for a couple of minutes, I gave him a hug, and then they were gone.

Years later, I attended a Kryon seminar in Los Angeles. While listening to a lecture on Indigo Children, I suddenly remembered Jombi, and it occurred to me that he was an Indigo. Everything made sense, enlightenment came full-blown, and I understood why Jombi did things his way. Another thing came up during that seminar, about one minute after the truth about Jombi floated into my brain. That was that his karate mentor was one of those Indigo kids who was born too early in this time to retain the Indigo persona. And of course, that mentor was me.

Remember Ali in the kitchen with all the pots and pans? (We're still thinking about it. Let's clone him and send him to kitchens all over America! Only kidding. Don't send us letters.) He was the one who seemed to know where everything belonged. Perhaps he should meet Beatrix, the two-year-old towel master.

Quick Fix in the Kitchen
Grace Koh

I've been meaning to write for some time now about my three-year-old daughter, Beatrix. She was born two weeks early, and she fussed and fretted each time we tried to put her to bed. She slept very little and wanted to be in the thick of things from day one. She wanted attention *all* the time, and you'd better deliver 100 percent or else! She was royalty all right, and the sooner we understood that, the easier it was for us to look after her! She quickly got bored of lying down on her back, and even before she was three months old, she was already clawing at her knees, trying to sit up!

When she was almost two, she wandered into the kitchen where I was preparing her lunch. She started to play with the hand towel that was on a hook. She asked why I had wound a piece of rubber band on it, and I explained that since the hooks weren't curved upward enough, the towel kept dropping off each time I wiped my hands. So I had wound a piece of rubber band around the hook, hoping to provide some "grip" for the towel and therefore keep it from falling off. (It still didn't work too well.)

Beatrix was quiet for a while and then piped up: "How about this, Mommy?" I took a look and saw that she had removed the rubber band, placed the loop of the towel on the hook, and then simply stretched the rubber band across *two* hooks. Believe me, that towel stayed on the hook until I removed it! Such a simple and yet effective solution! Can you blame anyone for cherishing their Indigo so?

What section about wisdom would be complete without proverbs from children, or things we've learned from them? What follows has been widely distributed on the Internet, so you might have already seen some of these statements.

Let's start with proverbs from children—wise sayings from the mouths of teenie-weenie adults.

Proverbs from the Indigos
Unknown Author. Source: The Internet

"Never trust a dog to watch your food." (Patrick, 10)

"When your dad is mad and asks you, 'Do I look stupid?' don't answer." (Hannah, 9)

"Never tell your mom her diet's not working." (Michael, 14)

"Stay away from prunes." (Randy, 9)

"Never pee on an electric fence." (Robert, 13)

"Don't squat with your spurs on." (Noronha, 13)

"Don't pull Dad's finger when he tells you to." (Emily, 10)

"When your mom is mad at your dad, don't let her brush your hair." (Taylia, 11)

"Never allow your three-year-old brother in the same room as your school assignment." (Traci, 14)

"Don't sneeze in front of Mom when you're eating crackers." (Mitchell, 12)

"Puppies still have bad breath even after eating a Tic-Tac." (Andrew, 9)

"Never hold a Dustbuster and a cat at the same time." (Kyoyo, 9)

"You can't hide a piece of broccoli in a glass of milk." (Armir, 9)

"Don't wear polka-dot underwear under white shorts." (Kellie, 11)

"If you want a kitten, start out by asking for a horse." (Lauren, 9)

"Don't pick on your sister when she's holding a baseball bat." (Joel, 10)

"When you get a bad grade in school, show it to your mom when she's on the phone." (Alyesha, 13)

"Never try to baptize a cat." (Eileen, 8)

This is a popular list called "Things I've Learned from My Children (Honest and No Kidding")." This came from the Internet, but was listed as "from an anonymous mother in Austin, Texas." So if *you* are that mother, let us know!

What a Mother Learned from Her Children
Unknown Author. Source: The Internet

- A king-size water bed holds enough water to fill a 2,000-square-foot house, four inches deep.

- If you spray hair spray on dust bunnies and run over them with Rollerblades, they can ignite.

- A three-year-old's voice is louder than 200 adults in a crowded restaurant.

- If you hook a dog leash over a ceiling fan, the motor isn't strong enough to rotate a 42-pound boy wearing Batman underwear and a Superman cape. It *is* strong enough, however, to spread paint on all four walls of a 20-by-20-foot room.

- You should not throw baseballs up when the ceiling fan is on.

- When using the ceiling fan as a bat, you have to throw the ball up a few times before you get a hit. A ceiling fan can hit a baseball a long way.

- The glass in windows (even double-pane) doesn't stop a baseball hit by a ceiling fan.

- When you hear the toilet flush and the words "Uh-oh," it's already too late.

- Brake fluid mixed with Clorox makes smoke, and lots of it.

- A 6-year-old can start a fire with a flint rock, even though a 36-year-old man says that it can only be done in the movies.

- A magnifying glass can start a fire even on an overcast day.

- Certain Legos will pass through the digestive tract of a four-year-old.

- The words *Play-Doh* and *microwave* should never be used in the same sentence.

- Super Glue is forever.

- No matter how much JELL-O® you put in a swimming pool, you still can't walk on water.

- VCRs do not eject peanut butter and jelly sandwiches even though TV commercials show they do.

- Garbage bags do not make good parachutes.

- Marbles in gas tanks make lots of noise when driving.

- You probably don't want to know what that odor is.

- Always look in the oven before you turn it on. Plastic toys do not like ovens.

- The fire department in Austin, Texas, has a five-minute response time.

- The spin cycle on the washing machine does not make earthworms dizzy. It will, however, make cats dizzy.

- Cats throw up twice their weight when dizzy.

Here are some proverbs, but with a twist. You know the common ones such as "Better to be safe than sorry"? Here, again from the Internet, is Indigo wisdom. The beginnings of well-known proverbs were given to children in a first-grade class. The teacher asked the children to supply the rest.

Proverbs
Unknown Author. Source: The Internet

- *Better to be safe than . . .* punch a fifth-grader.

- *Strike while the . . .* bug is close.

- *It's always darkest before . . .* daylight savings time.

- *Never underestimate the power of* . . . termites.

- *You can lead a horse to water but* . . . how?

- *Don't bite the hand that* . . . looks dirty.

- *No news is* . . . impossible.

- *A miss is as good as a* . . . mister.

- *You can't teach an old dog new* . . . math.

- *If you lie down with dogs, you'll* . . . stink in the morning.

- *Love all, trust* . . . me.

- *The pen is mightier than the* . . . pigs.

- *An idle mind is* . . . the best way to relax.

- *Where there's smoke, there's* . . . pollution.

- *Happy is the bride who* . . . gets all the presents.

- *A penny saved is* . . . not much.

- *Two's company, three's* . . . the Musketeers.

- *Don't put off till tomorrow what* . . . you put on to go to bed.

- *Laugh and the whole world laughs with you, cry and* . . . you have to blow your nose.

- *None are so blind as* . . . Stevie Wonder.

- *Children should be seen and not* . . . spanked or grounded.

- *If at first you don't succeed* . . . get new batteries.

- *You get out of something what you* . . . see pictured on the box.

- *When the blind leadeth the blind . . .* get out of the way.

- *Better late than . . .* pregnant.

Nancy Shea has three Indigos, and she's about to grace us with two stories via her poetry. Our favorite story, however, is about her boy during his "kindergarten aptitude test." She says this story would not fit into the poems below.

During the test, there were two questions that he treated in an unusual manner. First, he was asked to label the human body on an outline of it. Normally this results in the labeling of arms, legs, head, hands, and so on. Instead, he drew internal organs! From the parent chair in the hall, Nancy overheard the teacher say, "Interesting, and what do you use your bladder for?"

The second question? When he was asked to name something with wings, he answered, "Archangels." Our kind of kid!

Kindergarten Scholar
Nancy Shea

Petite for his age and with baby face features,
Meekly he entered to greet his new teacher.

She sensed at once that this was a creative child,
Then began to speak her manner mild.

"Now you're a kindergartner let's see what you know,
A couple fun tests and then you may go."

He knew all his parts including his knees,
He recited with eloquence his A B C's.

"What would happen if I dropped this ball?"
Well, gravity posed no problem at all.

These things can fly and these have four legs,
Then an A/B pattern with bright-colored pegs.

"Great!" she said, smiling at her young scholar.
Beaming with pride, he straightened his collar.

I have one more question, beside him she knelt.
"Please tell me what you have when ice melts."

"I'm not sure," he replied in a worried small voice.
So she rephrased the question to give him more choice.

She waited with the patience and poise of a dancer,
'Cause she knew in her heart, he had the right answer.

Then puffing his chest with the conviction of a king,
He confidently answered, "When the ice melts, it's
spring."

My Friend Johnny Joe
Nancy Shea

Johnny Joe was a wonderful boy.
Unfortunately hadn't yet learned to be coy.

He would often out loud speak his mind
Which frequently left his parents in a bind.

Here's one incident that happened to this lad
In church one Sunday with his mom and dad.

The pastor's wife entered wearing a large hat.
And right in front of Johnny is where she sat.

Silence is what his mom prayed for most.
But Johnny stood up and bellowed: "That hat is
GROSS!"

While the pastor's wife graciously tried to ignore us,
His dad replied cleverly: "You're right son, it's enormous."

In our first book, we talked about how much trouble the Indigo Children have in school. We called them "system busters" and told you that they were eventually going to break the system. After the release of *The Indigo Children,* that's exactly what started happening. The kids have become smarter than the tests and are beginning to complain en masse about how bad the questions are. This is made worse by a system that often demands a scoring curve as a criterion for federal funding and school accreditation.

In June of 2000, *Time* magazine highlighted this very problem in an article called, "Is That Your Final Answer?" They said, "Educators have had to dumb down their lessons to teach the often picayune factoids covered by the exams." *Time* also reported that "in Illinois, 200 students claimed they flunked the test on purpose."

This situation put teachers between a rock and a hard place. The system demanded that they improve the students' test scores, and the students wouldn't take the tests! What happened? It made news. Again, according to *Time:* "In the past few months alone, allegations of teacher-assisted cheating have roiled schools in California, Florida, Maryland, New York and Ohio." In a *Time* sidebar article entitled "Dumb Questions for Bright Kids?" the statement was made: "The revolt by educators against what they consider inappropriate testing has now reached even the arena where the very best students compete."

So, did the teachers suddenly become dishonest? Hardly. If we haven't said so before, we consider those in education to be passionate about children, underpaid, underappreciated, and warriors for children's education. Many are facing this same dilemma in various degrees—do they satisfy an aging system, or do they concede that the kids really do need something new? It's a tightrope walk, and perhaps as parents, we should take a moment to honor the teachers all over the world who are facing this challenge.

Meanwhile, what does this intellectual and political struggle look like to children? Here's the short story of Lee, an eight-year-old who doesn't know anything about politics or the system. He just *feels* it. From London comes the story of the "Automatic Kid."

The Automatic Kid
Sharon Marshall

Following your request for new stories about Indigo Children, I thought you might like to hear an interesting analogy provided by my eight-year-old son, Lee. Lee is fascinated by machines and has often told me that he *is* (rather than *will be*) a great inventor/scientist.

A couple of days ago, I asked him why he was so unhappy at school. He explained that it was because they wanted him to operate *manually,* and he was *automatic.* I asked him to elaborate. He went on to say that to be operated manually meant "to be controlled," and that's what the teachers wanted to do to him.

I remarked that machines could only be automatic if they had been preprogrammed, and so they still needed someone to control them at the start. But Lee replied (as if it was obvious), "No, it's different. I *am* pre-programmed. I *know* what I need to do, and I don't need to be controlled by teachers."

What can I say?

Thank you for the opportunity to share my boy's latest gem with you, and for taking the time to write *The Indigo Children,* which makes sense of everything (including my own childhood!).

Kids are wizards with electronic equipment. Go ahead—ask your children to keep the numbers from flashing on your VCR, or to program the thing. They can!

You might expect the following from a kid in elementary school, but how about a child under two? Okay . . . she didn't program the VCR . . . but maybe when she's three?

Children Who "Just Know How"
Jere Neal

I have a beautiful little granddaughter who's about to turn two. There have been many incidents where she has said or done something, and we said, "Where in the world did she get that?" She seems to be a very intelligent child (but of course, I'm biased). She is also very willful. As the book [*The Indigo Children*] says, "Self-worth is not a big issue," and "They come into the world with a feeling of royalty." Right away, as an infant, she let us know in no uncertain terms what she liked and disliked! She has her own opinion about everything, but she can also be very sweet, loving, and knows how to "play" the whole family, even the day-care staff!

Two incidents that come to mind most recently are: (1) When she was only 18 months old, her mother was letting her watch the *Little Mermaid* video while she was getting ready in the other room. My granddaughter didn't really want to watch that video at that time. She wanted to watch *Lady and the Tramp.* However, her mother was tired of that one, so she said, "Just watch *Mermaid,* and I'll be right out."

When she came out of the other room, my granddaughter was happily sitting on the couch watching *Lady and the Tramp!* She had taken the other video out of the machine and had inserted the new one correctly and started it. Her mother was stunned!

(Authors' note: Okay . . . so kids can mimic stuff, right? But we want to remind you that this little girl had to find the "eject" button, then take the tape out properly, put the other in far enough for the sensing motor to "seat" it, and then press the "start" button. We would have been stunned, too.)

(2) Recently (remember, she's not yet two) several members of the family were sitting around the living room discussing Christmas. My mother-in-law said she had gotten my granddaughter a "T-E-N-T" (spelling it) for her bed. My granddaughter just looked up and said what we all heard to be "tent," and went on quietly watching

TV. We just all looked at each other, not quite believing what we had just heard.

Okay, if a toddler already knows about the VCR, how about an 11-year-old? This particular boy is designing computers between math problems!

Solar Powered, Voice Activated
Marcia Pack

First, let me thank you for your book, *The Indigo Children.* What a revelation and enlightenment it has been to me. It seems that I have a houseful of Indigos! We have five children, and my husband and I have decided that they're all Indigos—the older ones being the forerunners, complete with the unique set of challenges described in your book.

My warm and fuzzy story (only one of them) has to do with my now 11-year-old boy, Kyle. When he was in the third grade, Kyle was doing poorly in school; his writing skills, processing, and achievement scores were far below where they should have been. Kyle acted-out, and very often "reacted" to someone else by hitting them. His reactions were often overreactions to what had happened. Kyle is a brilliant child, but he couldn't stay on task and was very easily distracted.

His IQ score came in at 129, but his performance score was only 105, indicating a "learning disability, since there's more than a 20-point spread between the two. I scheduled a meeting with his three teachers, as Kyle could not complete homework, was very disorganized, and "forgot" everything.

We were discussing a particular math paper he had done in school, and he had only completed two or three problems on the entire thing. We adults all puzzled over this when I suggested that we call Kyle in and ask him about it. He came in, I showed him the math paper, and asked him, "Kyle, you didn't finish this paper. What were you thinking of instead of the assignment? Were you looking outside? Was another child distracting you? What?"

Kyle studied it closely for a few minutes and responded with, "Oh, *this* paper? Ohhhh . . . that's when I was designing my solar-powered, voice-activated computer so you could use the computer hands-free even when the power goes off, and you wouldn't need a mouse!" Then he reached into his bag and produced a schematic for said computer!

The teachers and I sat dumbfounded, looking at each other, and one of them said, "Well, Mrs. Pack, what do you suggest?" I just began laughing and threw up my hands and said, "That's why I'm here. *You* are the experts, and that's *my* question."

There have been many other "Indigo incidents," but my husband and I have laughed over this one so many times that I just had to e-mail you about it.

In the first Indigo book, we told parents that the best thing they could do was to: (1) respect their children as friends, and (2) give them choice. Many have reported that the best method for parenting Indigos was to treat them as adults in small bodies who are trying to "remember" everything. You're just helping them with rediscovery. Would you yell at a friend who didn't want to eat when you did?

No. Then don't do it with children either. If you don't treat these kids with respect, they will often come down on you in ways that aren't childlike. Take, for instance, the experience of Doris, a mother of four.

Who Is This Kid Anyway?
Doris Crompton

I have four children ages 5, 8, 11, and 12. As I was getting more familiar with the Indigo material, I started to understand my children a lot better. Before, I could not understand why they weren't responding to the way I was trying to discipline them. You probably all agree that the old way, the way used in the '50s and '60s on us, is not working anymore.

When I got angry with my kids sometimes, I noticed that they would look at each other and ask, "What's wrong with Mom?" Sometimes they would say to me, "You sure are cranky today, Mom." I soon found out that their energy level was different. They didn't get intimidated in front of me like I used to when I was a kid facing one of my parents. At times, when my emotions were out of hand and my children responded as they did, I felt as if I was being the toddler and they were the more mature ones.

Once, one of my sons looked me straight in the eye and told me in a strong voice, "Mom, you are *not* allowed to talk to me this way." One part of me could have felt offended (hey—I'm the grown-up here), but the other part of me said, "He is absolutely right." I apologized. There was no arrogance in his voice or malice in his look, but there *was* a certain dignity that moved me.

I learned my lessons, after trial and error. These children need to be treated with respect. They are beautiful beings of light, and the more I think this way, the better my relationship with them has become. It was almost a magical transformation; they respond so much better when they're treated the way they ought to be. Only love can be used. Fear, threats, and all the old tools of the past can be buried forever, for they work no more.

We would like to close this chapter regarding wise children with an essay by an educator; a series of very short essays from children 9, 10, and 11 years old; and then a poem.

Justine Turner is an elementary school teacher in California. You might be interested in what this educator is thinking about today's kids.

They Aren't Like Us
Justine Turner

Indigos don't respond to guilt tactics common to earlier family and social structures. They don't react well to coercion, "talking down," punishment, "time-outs," "no recess," or to any of the normal social norms that teachers or families have used as a means of inflicting discipline. They don't respond to the school principal (the big boss) like we did, or even smackings like we did. There are very few measures they don't lash back at and refuse to get in line with. First, they don't get back into line. And second, there *is* no line!

What Indigos do respond to is respect—respect for who they are as wise individuals and as children, and respect for their problems, which are just as overwhelming to them as they are to us. They respond to respect for their choices and their power. They make good decisions, with help, and they struggle mightily to have their power make a difference and be important. They *are* important. They will soon be in charge of our world. That alone demands respect from us.

I no longer see teaching as a place for numbers and rules and structure. It's no longer a place where success can be measured solely on test scores or multiplication tables. What's the point? Indigos have tools and resources we never dreamed of (well, some of us did!), and in the future, they will have even more tools that we haven't dreamed of yet. What they need is to experience the joy of learning, exploring; and reading about history, math, ecology, and earth and physical sciences so they can create their own dreams.

They need to learn math, absolutely, but they need to learn it in a way that encourages them to play with shapes and patterns and twists and formulas—to use it as basic knowledge and then leave the checkbook balancing, once they understand it, to the computer. They need to know how to read for the joy of reading and to see things in a different way.

I think that teaching can be, now more than ever, a place for raising *human beings*. There's an opportunity for every teacher, for 183 days a year at most, to make a difference in these children's lives—so we can all create a better world. School is a place where these kids can understand that they won't always have to be squished under adults who do not see them for who they are. Their power must come from the inside. School may be where they fall apart, and school can be a place where someone will care enough to listen, understand, tell stories, laugh, and help put them back together. It's a place where these kids can see that they make a difference not only to others, but also to themselves. This is what they respond to.

These children speak with a great deal of wisdom. They struggle with insecurity, with growing up, with powerlessness, with learned helplessness, and with social inequity. They struggle with being different, with being a boy or a girl, with having friends or not, or being good at sports or not. There's nothing that they speak of that we can't understand if we listen. There's nothing they're feeling that we haven't felt sometime in our lives. That seems to be what they need and respond to now—the fact that we feel what they feel, which means that they're not alone. It is then that they can learn. It is then that they put forth the effort to see what we have to offer as adults, since we've taken the interest in what they have to offer.

That's the point where we teachers can fit in adjectives and addition, zoology and time zones. We have the profoundly exquisite chance at that juncture to teach subjects such as history in a way that enlightens them about the past, as well as giving them choices for the future. We can teach science that tells them about the workings of the earth and her special places, and we can teach about government and the history of religious differences so these kids can see alternate ways of thinking about things. This may look like teaching for *their* future, but it really is for *ours.*

Watch these Indigos with smaller children. Watch how they nurture and touch. Watch how they guide and tell and show. Laugh to yourself when you see your words come out of their mouths. Listen to them whine that the little ones don't follow directions! Smile, and know you're being blessed. Know that they have heard you and have appreciated what you said enough to use it. Pray you have said it well. Laugh with them when you point out how you feel and how they feel. Hurt when something hurtful comes out, and understand that not everyone in their lives is there in peace. Watch their power as they turn a little brother or sister sway from a mistake they made, like being "bad" in school or joining a gang. It's sometimes only through our young people that even younger kids can be supported and saved. Watch them with other adults. It doesn't matter whether that adult is a construction worker or a firefighter or a principal. What matters is the respect they show to all people. We must teach what respect looks like and feels like. These kids need to know what to do to get it and how to give it.

They know they will take over. They know they will have big choices, and they're scared. To the last of them, they want to do their best, whether they're a baseball star or a scientist. They want to make a difference, to be special, and to be heard. They *want* to do the right thing— every one of them.

They won't always *do* the right thing. Some are lost— very lost. Some will have many years of feeling like a misfit before finding themselves. Some have the power right now, and the challenge will be to use it well. Not all will, of course. Some have it so quietly that it's almost a secret. Others will go down in flames. But every one of them should have the chance to be guided by us in a way that encourages them to be their best. This helps them see themselves "making it" so they can continue their own dreams of greatness.

What may look to us like children writing about pipe dreams and fantasies are really young adults trying to find their way and finding their power. When you listen, listen for that. When you talk, talk to them of greatness, and speak with intelligence. When you structure, do so cleanly, honestly, and with boundaries that they understand and that you stick to. That is respect. That they understand. That they will respond to.

Now it's time to hear from the children in Justine's class about what they see for themselves. She asked her children to write short essays about what they wanted to be, and what they wanted to do in the future.

Ask yourself whether *you* thought about being a humanitarian when you were nine. Probably not. Take a look at the quandary of normal children's dreams, and the obvious Indigo tendency toward being the "peacemaker." One child can't decide between basketball or being a pediatrician. His decision? To become a basketball pediatrician!

We cleaned up the spelling to make it easier to read, but we left the grammar intact.

21 Precious Futures
From the Students

Justine: These are journaled writings done on January 23, 2001. The question given to the students surrounded the issues of new days, new beginnings, and what to do and be in this lifetime, starting today. I love these young people and this job!

STUDENT 1

What I want to do with my lifetime is to be a doctor. Or I might be a teacher. I want to be a helpful person. And I want to be a person that can be useful. The things that I am good at are school stuff like homework, math, and a little bit of history. The thing I want to work on is my personality. I want to be a good person to all the people. And sometimes I think about what I can do to make the world a better place.

STUDENT 2

When I grow up I'm going to be a president and give money to poor people and make peace on Earth and have no littering so I could make a better planet out of this place.

STUDENT 3

I want to take my lifetime and get the best education I can. I want to be a cop when I grow up because I want to be just like my grandpa. And I want to be a daddy. I want to be a nice person who helps a lot of people. I want to be the best person I could be. I am good at math, I try not to fight with someone. And I'm good at taking care of my baby sister.

STUDENT 4

I would want to publish a book or work in a good career in a place that nobody would yell at me. I want to be a person that would be nice and respectful or a person that works with others. A person that would give chances or second chances. I am good at making paper boats or good at making paper snowflakes. I would want to work on my health, stay better and not get sick.

STUDENT 5

When I grow up I would like to help people make their dreams to come true. I would also put a smile on everyone's face. I would also like everybody to agree on things. If I could tell everyone to vote because their words count too. I would like for everyone to feel equally. I would like everyone to retire on something good. I also want to be a policeman. I would like to be a nice gentleman.

STUDENT 6 (an organized kid!)

Every day is a new life. I'm going to do the following each day:

1. Be a person who stands up and tries to do something nice.

2. I am good at math/spelling in my class.

3. I want to work at a school and tell the thing about myself, like "I like pets and math."

4. I want to start a new good day and say good morning to everyone.

5. I am going to be a teacher/a substitute, when I grow up.

6. I am good at writing and playing/smiling with my friends.

7. I like to do some things that are very fun at recess.

8. I am starting a new thing and that is going to my friend's house every day after school.

STUDENT 7

The first thing I am going to do is that: I want to help other people. The second thing I am going to do is that: If I ever forget to do my homework, tell Ms. Turner the truth. The third thing that I am going to do is: I am going to help my sister, Mom, Dad, or cousin. The fourth thing I am going to do is: I want to study to be a skater or a teacher. I want to be good at stuff. I want to be a nice person that does not scream. I want to be an artist. I want to help everybody in the world. I want to be good.

STUDENT 8 (Give this kid a subscription to *Animal World* immediately!)

I have a dream that one day I would be a veterinary assistant. I would like to care for dogs, cats, pigs, and all kinds of animals. I would like to see different kinds of animals. I would like to make animals feel better, as better as can be. I just love Africa, and that is where most animals are. If animals are hurt bad I would be there. I would be a service to anyone who is a veterinarian. I love animals very much.

STUDENT 9

I want to take my lifetime and get a good education. So the things that I didn't get before, if I have another choice, and pay more attention to it and so I know how to use it. So I could get a good job I enjoy. I want to be a pediatrician or basketball pediatrician, because I like helping people. Basketball, because I like shooting hoops. I feel I'm more free playing it. I want to be a more responsible or helpful person in the world. I'm good at helping people and playing basketball and schoolwork. I would like to work on being nicer to fellow students or others and take time to read and write neater.

STUDENT 10 (complete with drawings around the paper)

With my new life I would like to be president. I would give food to the poor and hungry. I would give them a house to live in. I would like to be nice to everyone. The thing I am good at is being nice to everyone. I need to work on how to be president. I want to be great.

STUDENT 11

This is my lifetime. The thing that I want to do with it is to know that I could do anything with my life if I set my mind to it. The kind of person that I want to be is the kind of person who cares and could get my responsibilities taken care of. The thing that I think that I am good at is cheerleading because I take classes on it and I get really good compliments on it. The thing that I think that I am not good at is picking clothes to wear for school each day.

STUDENT 12

I want to work hard in school or try to be president of Mexico to make that place a better place. I'm good at soccer, racing games, and skateboards. I want to be better and smarter because my dad wants me to try harder. I don't want to scream a lot because it makes me sound like a bad person. I want to be best at things like school and games. I want to be a good person and grow up to be an advisor who helps people.

STUDENT 13

I want to go to college and get good grades so I could be a police officer. I only want to give a ticket to bad people, like if they kidnapped a little boy or a little girl and we found out who was the kidnapper. I hope I don't get shot like the police officer but I forgot his name. I am a little good at driving but sometimes I crash. I want to learn how to drive more. And how to handle guns when I grow up. I want to be a police officer because I want to help people that are almost dying and to put a person in jail who kidnapped a little girl or boy.

STUDENT 14

I want to help people who are down and I want to be rich. I want to be 100% cute. I want Martin Luther King to still be alive. I want people from all over the world to grab hands and look that person in the eye and say "You are my sister." I want to make friends with everyone. I want my mom to be happy.

STUDENT 15

I want to be a person who helps people when they need it. I still want to go to school. I want to study more about history. I want to practice more on spelling. I want to do math. I want to go to college so I could get a better job and take care of my family. I am good at playing foursquare. I am also good at doing my homework but I forget to bring it to school.

STUDENT 16

I would try my hardest in school. I would finish college for three years. I would visit Ms. Turner. I would be a fighter pilot. I would buy a dog. I want to be a marine biologist. I would be best friends with Cesar and Richard. I would finish my homework. I would get a leopard spot. (An award given for good work in class.)

STUDENT 17

What I would do with my lifetime: I will teach students or play pro basketball. I want to be someone who is involved in the church. I am good at subjects in school, games, and sports. I want to work on being neater and even better at basketball. I also think that I should work on getting my handwriting neater. I say that every school year and it always gets a little better.

STUDENT 18

I would like to try harder to work on my singing group and my modeling. To try and become rich so I could buy my own land and my own machine and I'm going to have security and own private pool and my own private party-house just for kids and be a nice, kind person.

STUDENT 19

I would want to be the president and I would change the world by making new laws. And make the fines bigger and no wars, cause people die.

STUDENT 20

I will start a new life today. I would like to be a person who helps people and treats others the way you want to be treated. I want to be nice. And I want to be intelligent and the things I'm going to work on are my people skills. What I would like to do with my life is to be the most helpful I can be and go to college and be a successful singer and dancer and when I retire I will help with community service.

STUDENT 21

I want to make the right decisions on what needs to be done. I want to be a person who can change people's lives from sorrow to happy, happy, joy, joy! I want to be able to prove to all people that you can be anything you want to be, and you can do what you want to do. I am good at cleaning. I am good at singing. I am good at a lot of little things and a couple of big things but there's only a couple things that really I love to do and that I'm really good at and that's helping people and singing. The things I want to work on changing is expressing my feelings and spreading my unhappiness to others when I'm upset. But I want to keep everything else about me the same because I like me. My new year's resolution is to

**be a better learner and listen to the teacher. I would like
to be a pro-soccer player. I don't want to always get mad
at somebody. I want to spend more time with my family.
When I grow up I would like to be a business person.**

We've given you only part of the communicated
thoughts offered by the students in the above essays. What
we couldn't show you was the handwriting (good and bad),
the drawings doodled around the words, and the obvious differences in levels of learning. Some students had perfect
spelling, while others had a difficult time. But the dreams
were similar.

Most of all, we couldn't show you something very
personal—the responses by Justine Turner, the teacher
who asked the questions, who made comments on every
one of the small pieces of paper the students gave her. Like
so many other dedicated teachers, it was obvious that she
was a master psychologist, mom, and educator all rolled
into one. She congratulated the children (no matter how
bad the spelling or grammar was). The exercise was about
dreaming and imagination, and she graded on how well
they grasped the concept of sharing this personally. She
patted them on the back and wrote words such as "Great!"
and "Please come see me when you grow up." Justine is the
kind of teacher who is remembered for a lifetime.

We promised you a poem. This is from Jenny Marrs, a
mom with an Indigo Child with Down's syndrome. I think
you will see the wisdom of both the Indigo and the mom.

The Extra Within
Jenny Marrs

Each cell has an extra chromosome, so they say,
And all they can see is "There will be a delay."
A delay in development, "He won't walk before two."
A delay in his speech, "His words will be few."
A delay in cognition, "Will he read, will he write?"
The future predicted was not very bright.
He's proven them wrong about all of these things,
But that pales in comparison to the message he brings.
As an infant he had such an aura of love,
The warmth from his heart had to be from above.
His Granny once told us "I'm mysteriously drawn,
To the love that is quite special which is coming
    from John."
And who was he seeing in that spot in his room?
When he was laughing and cooing—I can only assume:
Was he talking with angels, were they causing his joy?
Were they already guiding this small baby boy?
Did they fill him with compassion and give him the gift
Of intuitively knowing when one needs a lift?
I've seen him so often just enter a room
Bringing sunshine and happiness, where before there
    was gloom.
His heart is wide open. He's genuine. He's true.
He has a charm and a sweetness which escapes very few.
A stranger once told us "Children will lose their wings,
At age seven or so they move on to more worldly things."
He said that my child has a much greater plan,
He'd be keeping his wings and that he's touched by
    God's hand.
He's still learning and growing, but he's closer than most

To achieving God's perfection, yet it's him we diagnose.
Is it we who are lacking that one chromosome
And the enlightenment which leads us to our heavenly
    home?
John's working so hard to learn all worldly things,
He reads and he writes, he loves school, and he sings.
He's speaking quite well, yet still a man of few words
Because only in silence can God's voice be heard.
So sit at his feet, and listen if you dare
For this little child has such wisdom to share.

"A young and vital child knows no limit to his own will,
and it is the only reality to him.
It is not that he wants at the outset to fight other wills,
but that they simply do not exist for him.
Like the artist, he goes forth to the work of creation,
gloriously alone."

— **Jane Harrison**, English classical scholar[1]

The Spiritual Indigos

We told you in the first Indigo book that the Indigo Children were very interested in God. Not only that, we also told you that they were sensitive to energy, saw and felt unusual things, and had opinions on what God might be, as well as who *they* (the kids) might be. This chapter is a combination of these things, as well as the weird and the spooky.

Is it possible that we've actually lived before? Perhaps it's just in our imagination. Right before the millennium shift, there were many articles in national magazines about religion. Since we were perceived to be at the edge of the Armageddon prophecy, there were a bunch of exploratory and informative reports on how major religions viewed the earth at the moment. A statement was made that "85% of the earth's population believes in the afterlife" (you have to take into account the millions of people who are Islamic, Hindu, and Buddhist). Our own observations, however, show us that while this may be true, most *do not* believe in the "*fore*-life." Especially those from Western cultures.

To us, as metaphysical teachers, this doesn't make any spiritual sense. That means that somehow, through biological birth, you get an eternal soul. You didn't exist and suddenly, POOF! —you're "forever." If you did indeed live before, we doubt that we will ever be able to prove it any more than others can disprove it. Proving concepts such as heaven and hell are in the same category, and even the Pope got into the act last year by defining them as not actually being real (**www.vatican.va**). We're not evangelical, so it's not something we ask you to believe. Instead, it remains a spiritual mystery, known only by God . . . or perhaps the Indigos? In other words, it's never going to be solved for us, but we can think about it and decide for ourselves. Spiritual choice is the ultimate privilege of any human. It requires pure intent to ask God what's appropriate or not—something very personal and known at the heart level.

The interesting thing that's happening now is that Indigo Children all over the world are telling their parents who they "used to" be! This is so widespread that it's a common thread of discussion at seminars and conferences that we attend. It happens way before the children can be exposed to any "past-life" dogma, and usually right after they begin to talk. As we previously acknowledged, many parents are frightened by this kind of talk, and are taking their children to the priests or others in their church who might help get "the devil" out of them.

If your belief system really isn't in tune with this past-life talk, then here is what we recommend: Don't be afraid for your kids or for yourselves. They're not possessed. Honor them with patience, even if you may not believe what they're saying. Parents are reporting that much of this type of discussion often subsides by the time the children are eight to ten years old. Don't belittle them or make them "wrong." This will only separate you from your children. Take them to the church of your choice, and watch them enjoy the experience. These kids are very smart spiritually, and many will find the church experience to be something they look forward to. They will feel the love in the assemblage, and they relate to the feelings of being part of something spiritually profound for all—something that is very close to "home" for them somehow.

Some parents who don't go to a church (or synagogue or other place of worship) have reported that the children want to! So they've given their children a "tour" of the churches in their neighborhood when the children are of a certain age. Each Sunday (or Saturday, if appropriate), they visit a different place of worship. The children sit in the services and observe and "feel." Then after a few weeks, the parents ask the children to decide where they'd like to attend.

We feel that this is the most honoring situation we've ever heard of regarding the Indigos. It respects their discernment abilities and gives them freedom of choice. It doesn't force them into the religious mold their parents are in (or perhaps the parents of the parents). Instead, it's a magnificent example of Indigo parenting. Believe us, the children respond positively! Of course, the unspoken sentiment here is that the adults will also attend the church with the kids until the children are old enough to be dropped off and picked up. However, most adults have found the experience very rewarding and bonding for them and their kids. They also tend to meet quality friends at these gatherings.

Spiritual children make wonderful zealots for God. This is not a negative statement, but a fact. They feel close to God energy and often tell you about it. If allowed, they'll even start their own churches eventually, if yours don't suit them. They are sensitive to illogical spiritual beliefs, and to people who say one thing and do another. They sense the energy of deceit and know when a person is unbalanced. They expect integrity from grown-ups and react when they don't get it. Even in the Middle East, where children are in camps being taught to "rage in God's name," they are responsive to a lack of integrity in adults. There's no rule that says that Indigos will all think one way or the other. Instead, we're noticing that they respond to "God talk" more profoundly than any of us did at their age. Nancy Tappe (the woman who originally "saw" and reported the Indigo Children), tells us more about the psychology of this phenomenon in an upcoming chapter.

From birth to about age eight, profound things come out of the mouths of Indigos about God and humanity. Sometimes they see angels or magic friends (by the way, from what parents tell us, the children say that some of their pets do, too!). This is different from our own fantasies as children, as documented by many child psychologists. In our day, we saw what the TV and movies suggested we see. We had Peter Pan or Tinkerbell as our friends. These children have no model for what they're reporting. It's out of this world, and not (yet) in movies or on TV.

At a time when physicists are now reporting that the center of all matter has at least 11 dimensions—and that we only "see" four (it's called String Theory), isn't it conceivable that there's a greater unseen universe *out there* and that pieces of interdimensional Divinity are with us? Suddenly science is admitting that we're not seeing everything, and there may be much more to see! Are there angels? Could the children be able to see interdimensionally for the first few years of their lives, since perhaps they were just "there" a few years ago? What about their "pre-birth" experiences?

This is not a forum that will answer those questions. Instead, it's one that will look at what the children have said or experienced. Then you can ponder these universal questions for yourselves. Isn't it interesting that the children might be the key to showing us Divine truth? "Out of the mouth of babes . . ." is becoming a more profound statement than ever before.

What do you get when you ask children about God? When Kathryn Hutson asked her four-year-old (on tape), "What is God?" This was his response: "A huge, shining ball of light with spikes coming out of it—it touches everything and feels good!" (She still has the tape.)

Brian Coleman was walking on the beach one day with his son, Davis. They noticed how the sun came through the clouds shining down on the water.

Davis asked his dad, "Do you know what I call those spots on the water?"

"What?" replied Brian.

"I call those God spots."

"Oh. And what's the purpose of those God spots?"

"When people die, those beams of light are like elevators that bring the soul back up to heaven."

Notice that the child said "back up to heaven," as though perhaps this Earth life was an interruption in a heaven-life.

What about a child who actually tries to identify what went on before he got here? Listen to this story from Joanne Wisor about Greg, age four.

An Angel Named Robert
Joanne Wisor

We have an Indigo who is now nine. Greg has always talked about seeing angels. He has described them as being different colors, and has said that they even turn into animals and birds, like hawks and eagles, etc., when he's alone in his room. As we drive in the car, he'll say things like, "Mom, there's a brown angel in the car with us."

When Greg was four, he came down from bed one night (you know, the knack for delaying bedtime?) and told me a story about an angel that took care of him before he was born. He even told me the name. But when I was telling my husband later, I couldn't remember it.

About six months later, he came to us both and told the exact same story again. As soon as he said the name, I recognized it! He said that an angel named Robert Stoben had taken care of him before he was born. He said that Robert told him that he (Robert) had died in a car accident on the way to visit his grandparents. He then told us that Robert stayed with him until it was time to come here, so he went into my blood and stayed in my tummy until the doctor cut him out. (I had a C-section, and I don't think that he knew about that, or what it was.)

He talks less and less about these sorts of things as he gets older, but every now and again, he'll open up and tell us more about what he sees. I never push; I want what he has to say to be pure. I try to keep the door open, you might say, and try to answer his hundred questions a day (grin) as best I can. Some of them are doozies! Once he asked me, "Mom, way back when, when people drove cars like the Flintstones, did they speak English?" So you see, life is never dull in this house!

Again, we say that the Indigo children can often "see" right through you. Many parents have written about this. Here is one who compares what happened with her two-and-a-half-year-old son to a spiritual experience. Sometimes the kids do that to us.

Sensing True Feelings
Moneque LeBlanc

Rémi was about two and a half years old when one day he asked me, "Mama, are you angry?"

"No, I'm not angry," I replied calmly.

He repeated the same question twice, and each time I insisted that I wasn't.

A few days later, he asked me again if I was angry, and I reaffirmed that I was not. The second time he repeated the question, I thought to myself: *Why does he keep asking? Does he see or feel something that I don't?* I thought it was peculiar that the same scenario was repeating itself.

In my endeavor to bring up my son in the most honest fashion I was able, I knew that I had to be a true and pure example, so I turned inward to see how I was feeling. My heart *was* upset. It felt as if a battle or a storm was going on inside, and the agitation was pounding on the walls of my heart. I rationalized: "It's impossible for him to feel what's going on inside me, as I'm in control outwardly. My voice is calm, and I'm not manifesting any impatience!"

Being an extrovert, I had learned, until now, to manage some of my outward expressions of anger. I could control the pitch and tone of my voice and also heed my words, which I considered then to be quite a feat. But now, the questioning by my child was puzzling me.

All this went through my mind within the few seconds after my son asked me for the second time if I was angry. I noticed that I had denied three times his first round of questioning a few days back, and I felt like the Apostle Peter when he had denied three times his master, Jesus Christ. I didn't want to repeat this scenario. Confronting my desire to be honest with myself, I bent down, looked him straight in his eyes, and admitted: "Rémi, you're right! Mama's heart is upset, and I *am* angry inside, but not with you. I love you." I then hugged him, and my heart overflowed with love.

I was amazed by the insight of this 30-month-old child who could see right through me and detect my hidden feelings. I realized that he had guided me to look within and to get in touch with my feelings. I then thanked God for having this child come into my life. I knew within that this child, though not of my own flesh and blood, as we had adopted him when he was 11 days old, was meant to be with us and that we had "signed up" for this. I truly understood that being a parent was as much a learning experience as a teaching relationship. My heart was so grateful for this experience, and it moved me to tears. I savored the moment.

Okay, some of you are saying, "I don't think so . . . this is really for the spooky crowd . . . the Fruit-Loops-and-wind-chimes group. No truly logical person is going to believe this stuff."

If that's so, then educators and parents all over the world are becoming spooky. The Indigo experience, weird stuff and all, is happening with the same frequency within professional circles as it is with the "wind-chimes" group. That's because it's universal.

Let us introduce you to Constance Snow. She's an attorney in Florida, and she's currently writing a book called

How to Bring a Lawsuit with Love. Did you ever think you would see a profound consciousness shift in law? This is a good beginning. Constance has a personal knowledge of Indigo Children and has interviewed relatives of Indigos in order to acquire information about actual situations. She's a speaker and workshop leader who uses both legal and spiritual components in her presentations. We thought you might like to hear from her—someone who's in a profession that requires clear, logical, concise thought . . . with very few Fruit Loops.

Indigo Children
Constance Snow

Parents of the Indigos often find that raising them is a difficult task. The reason behind the difficulty is that they, the Indigos, do not conform to the usual rules by which their parents were indoctrinated. In addition, they're not easily controlled by shame, guilt, physical restraint, or punishment. Accordingly, they appear to match their "will" to that of their parents and other authority forms. As we know, they're not being "willful" for the sake of their own ego. They are, merely, asserting what they know is their own truth of being.

Because they're children, they are to be guided. Note that the parents' task here is to *guide* rather than to *control*. When recognized, supported, and nurtured, these children can provide the utmost joy to their families. Otherwise, they're capable of unparalleled assertion and constant testing of parental authority.

Since Indigos possess wisdom often greater than that of their parents, they may more easily communicate with their older family members such as grandparents. Parents may gain much insight on how to effectively deal with their remarkable children where they accommodate the counsel of their own parents. Through the Indigos, grand-parents will begin to become much more revered as wise counsel and sages within the family and society.

As parents and grandparents recognize that they have begotten an Indigo, they would be well advised to honor the child with great love and respect as one might a Christ Child. Then, commit to the support and nurtur-ing of the truth of the Being within the child's body. Become the intelligent steward of this powerful and beloved Indigo Child. Accepting the Indigo for who he/she is, especially when facing turbulence within the rearing process, requires conviction on the part of the adult. The parent must be convinced in mind and soul that the guidance of the Indigo Child is of utmost importance and a responsibility to be undertaken with joy.

Bringing lightness and relaxation into the process will provide an easier atmosphere within which to enjoy the day-to-day activities of family life. Give little or no attention to unpleasant circumstances, and focus on the truth of that which you acknowledge—which is the joy of contributing to the evolutionary process of the human race through raising a beautiful and powerful human being with love, compassion, and peace.

Indigo Children are extremely sensitive to energy and are capable of sensing vibrations from great dis-tances. If mainstream societal factors are attempting to diagnose and label your child in a less then acceptable manner (for example, ADD or ADHD), become well versed on the subject, look for the key to your child's method of learning and creativity, and seek review under alternative health considerations, especially treatment for hyper-sensitivity (allergy) to common food and environmental substances. Also remember that your emotions and stress play a large part in creating vibrations that may trigger hypersensitive reactions in your child.

Here's another story, this time from an educator in South Africa (yes, the Indigo experience is worldwide). Gabby van Heerden is one of those who feels that she's an Indigo, although she was born in 1970. She gave us details of her life, and indeed it sounds like it to us, too! There will actually be a chapter in this book on "older Indigos," so Gabby isn't alone in this feeling. She feels that her passion is to understand the Indigos of today and provide for them in the best way she can.

Gabby is in the classroom with these children, often many hours a day. Listen to what this educator has to say about choice, how to treat Indigos, and yes . . . even about angels and energy.

From an Educator in South Africa
Gabby van Heerden

I've just finished reading your book, and as always, I thank the Universe for sending the right information at the right time. So much has fallen into place!

The reason I'm giving you my life story is because events have guided me toward becoming an educator. Fight it, I did, because I detested school. I spent three years at college hating it almost as much as I did school, but in my fourth year, I decided to specialize in visual art education. It was as if I had come home.

Our rigid school system had no place for me, or the children that I was to work with. Visual art teaching opened a whole set of new doors, and I came to understand what education could really be like. I understood why I was doing what I was doing and valued the choice and freedom that it gave to me and my children.

This is really where my story begins. I'm lucky enough to teach art in Cape Town at a place called the Frank Joubert Art and Design Centre. We teach visual art from preschool to grade 12, and also run courses for teachers and other adults.

As I read your book, I realized how many Indigo Children have been sent my way and how fortunate I am to have them in my life. As a teacher, I am a system-buster and have never fit into the conventional teaching mode. I therefore seem to have drawn those children who are also system-busters in their own right. These are the children who require being treated as adults. I made the mistake of calling a class of children "my babies" once. One little boy looked at me and said, "I haven't been a baby for a long time, you know." I could see lifetimes in his eyes, and I apologized immediately.

I've also been blessed to have been sent an Indigo called Patricia. Patricia is now six years old and spent the first four years of her life attending a school for autistic children. She has now been mainstreamed, and she has been in my art class for just over a year. Patricia has the wisdom of years and will only do something if she can understand the reason why. She is often happiest on her own but will frequently place herself near a child who is in need of some kind of support. She is, therefore, never in the same place twice and rarely sits with the same group of children. I often see her communicating with the angels in a world of her own. I value and celebrate her independence and her unshakable understanding that she is exactly where she needs to be. My heart goes out to her when I think of her moving through our rigid school system (although it *is* changing), but I know that she's bringing many lessons to teachers and other children alike.

My Indigos will frequently speak of their angels or other beings in a matter-of-fact, everyday way. I often let them paint or draw their angels or friends, and am often awed at the beauty and detail of these pictures.

An art class is an ideal place for Indigos. Choice is required. Within a basic framework, children have to decide how to draw and what colors to use. There's no *right* or *wrong*, and the class dictates what we will do from week to week, how fast we will do it, and what the process will be.

As they come up, spiritual and life matters are discussed as everyday events. I often find that these children have a far better grasp of spiritual matters than their parents do. As I've progressed along my own spiritual path, my understanding has grown. I've been amazed at how very clearly these children understand spiritual concepts.

I work with two other Indigos, Mark and Bobbie. Both have been diagnosed with ADHD. Bobbie's parents were advised to put him on Ritalin but decided that it would not be right for their child. Bobbie is frequently in trouble with his peers because he has the ability to see the central issue in any given situation. This is often uncomfortable for the children and adults around him who would prefer not to hear the truth. Bobbie seems quite comfortable with the fact that he's following his own path, but at times he also seems to carry much frustration within him because he doesn't fit in.

Mark was on Ritalin, but his parents have wisely stopped that and have moved him to a more child-friendly school. He too is a system-buster and often brings lessons to me.

I always play music in my class, burn aromatherapy oils, and generally have gems and crystals around. I don't actively use them, but the children are welcome to "play" with them. Looking back on it, I now see how many of the Indigos have been drawn to the gems and crystals, or will tell the others to keep quiet so that they can listen to the music. They'll also be the ones who will come up to me and tell me that the music is terrible, and to please change it immediately!

I often wear a crystal around my neck, and some of my children will come and ask to wear it if they're feeling in need of a bit of support or if they've had a rough day at school. My crystal is often the first thing that Indigos will notice when they walk into my classroom. I do find that having a crystal or gem nearby—that they've chosen— will help to balance and focus an Indigo Child.

I wished that my parents had had your book when I was a child, but they also had the wisdom to let me follow my own path, even if they didn't understand it. I have lent the book to some of my colleagues so we can initiate a more broad-based understanding of our children.

Well, we've warmed up the "woo-woo" subject with an attorney and an educator. Now it's time to hear from some of the parents. Hang on to those wind chimes!

Indigos from the Other Side
Renee Weddle

It took my husband and me until I was almost 30 to decide that we wanted children. Our son, Jesse, was born in August of 1987; and our daughter, Mattea, was born in July of 1990.

Jesse was a delightful baby. He rarely cried, was very quiet, and even as a newborn did not like to be held a lot.

If he were held very much, he would cry until we put him in his crib and left the room. Many people remarked on how unusual this was, but I had never been around babies much and didn't think much about it.

When he was four or five years old, my son told me that he had been a ruler on another planet, there had been an earthquake and he had bumped his head on a rock, and his spirit had fallen into my tummy. When he told me this, I was not very spiritually aware, but my husband and I had always felt that we wanted to be open with our children, so we kept an open mind.

Another time, my son told me that he didn't feel his name should be Jesse, that in his last lifetime it had been Thomas! This led me to start reading about reincarnation. Many of the things Jesse shared with me have changed the way I look at life and at God.

Jesse was five or six when he started telling me that the people from his old planet were trying to talk to him. I asked him if he was able to talk to *them*, and he said he was, and he showed me how. He would just close his eyes and listen and tell me what he heard. I take it for granted that he can "read" people, but as he progresses into adolescence, this sensitivity seems to be growing, sometimes to the point where it causes him anxiety.

From an early age, Jesse could quite often read our thoughts. I feel that he has wisdom way beyond his years—at age five and six, he was trying to solve world-wide problems such as starvation and housing for homeless people. It got to the point where we took him to a child therapist because he was so serious and felt he needed to have more childlike fun. Often he said things like, "Mom, it's okay if we don't have money because we have all the gold in the sun, and that's all we need."

Mattea was born strong-willed and screaming. Even in the womb when my husband, Ed, would put his hand on my stomach, she would kick it off. She was a demanding baby, and that didn't change as she grew. When she was 18 months old and we said it was time to pick up toys, she would yell, "No!" and throw them across the room. After having a "quiet" Jesse, Mattea was quite the surprise!

When she was three or four, she asked me if I knew why she had chosen me to be her mother. I said I didn't know why (Jesse was six or seven at this time so I was getting the hang of being open to whatever they said). Mattea said, "I came here to teach you how to be goofy and silly." And she has, although I suspect she's still working on it!

We were positive that Mattea must have been royalty in another lifetime; she would choose her clothes by the feel of them (she preferred anything silky), and not understand if we wouldn't get her something because it was too expensive. She would wake up in the morning and yell from her bedroom, "I'm awake now. You can bring me breakfast in bed." Although I might do that once or twice a year for a treat, she would demand it daily and be upset when I wouldn't comply. She expected me to pick out her clothes, dress her, bathe her, etc., way beyond the age that children do this for themselves.

Fortunately we took the "Parenting with Love and Logic" class, which you recommend. We took it *twice,* and this helped us tremendously. Mattea is one Indigo who feels we should be at her beck and call, and although it has improved over the years, she still has that "air" about her at nine years old. She really does *not* understand why we can't have a maid or housekeeper and why she's expected to help with chores, clean her own room, and so on.

Mattea is totally loving, trusting, and strong-willed, which makes for an interesting combination. When she's angry, her wrath is palpable, but so is her love and caring, which extends to all living beings (she seems to have more maternal instincts than I do!).

She's very concerned about equality and fairness (not just for herself), and she's really sensitive to anyone's feelings being hurt, unless she's in a rage—then she's brutal. She's very verbal and has let me know several times in a fit of temper that she wished she had "chosen" another mother.

She sees and talks to fairies and gnomes and builds them places to play outside and places to sleep in her bedroom. From an early age, Mattea has been able to sense when a person is hurting, either physically or emotionally. More than once, Ed or I have sat quietly with some kind of ache, and she has come up and laid hands on us awhile and then asked if it felt better.

I could go on and on about both my kids. They are endlessly fascinating to me. When Ed and I decided to have children, this is *not* what I envisioned. This is more challenging and not at all what I expected, but I would not trade these two special beings for anything.

I've often felt that they've been more like teachers to me than I have been to them. I have come to the conclusion that the most I can do is love them, guide them, and respect them for the things they teach me. They have both expressed frustration when Ed and I cannot answer their spiritual questions, but we do try to help them find the answers. Of course, it is Mattea that insists that we *do* know the answers and we're keeping them from her on purpose. This happened when she was hearing voices in her bedroom and seeing flashes of light. I read books that I thought might have answers, and I consulted friends. When I suggested that the voice could possibly be her spirit guide, she was very frustrated because she felt I should know.

Thank you so much for writing *The Indigo Children.*

Recognition of Family
Anne Saunders

I'm an Aussie mum with three Indigos.

Jessica was 20 to 22 months old when she walked past a photo of my grandmother, who hadn't been on this earth for over ten years. Jessica pointed to the photo and said, "I know that lady!" We hadn't spoken of "Nana" to Jess at that stage and were dumbfounded when Jessica said, in a tone that left no doubt that she thought we were totally stupid for not knowing, "She visited me when I was in Mummy's belly."

I didn't doubt it, and curiously asked numerous questions. Jess put her little two-year-old pout on and crossed her arms, indignantly refusing to answer any more silly questions.

I have two girls, seven and three years old, and a seven-month old son who is showing more will than both of the girls combined. So I am once again eagerly awaiting your next book!

"They Are Not Dead!"
Susan Saunders

I live with my soulmate, Wayne, who has a six-year-old daughter named Samantha. The first time we sensed that she was connected was about a year ago. Wayne had picked up a couple of new books from which to read her bedtime stories. This was unknown to Sammy. She was jumping on the bed, and Wayne told her it was time to start settling down. She continued bouncing and then stopped cold, looked at Wayne, and said, "Crystal [her first angel] said if I would calm down and go to bed that you have new stories to read to me!"

A few weeks later while traveling across town in the car, Sammy began to ask about her grandfather. When Wayne told her that he had died when she was 12 months old, she paused and said in a somewhat stern tone, "Daddy, he's not dead—and neither is Grandma [who had died a year prior]. They both talk to me, and they talk to you, too, but you just don't listen."

She also loves playing with the animals in Animal Heaven. She claims you don't necessarily go back to heaven when you die. She said that she knows why she came back: "To send love to everyone." She has stated, "I knew I made a mistake coming back to Earth when I was in Mommy's tummy. I told God that I had changed my mind and wanted to go back home, but He said it was too late."

Sammy's very frustrated that she can't fly unless she's sleeping. She told me that I was her mother in heaven once. One evening at dinner, she casually asked where kangaroos live and asked if Indians lived there, too. She remembered being a boy and falling in love with the

Indian chief's daughter where there are kangaroos. There was much detail related to this story.

Sammy explains that she uses her wings to fly, but she also uses a bubble to protect her. She said it's so easy; you just think of where you want to go and you're there. There is one planet that is so windy that it's really hard to get in. But when you do, everything is shimmering gold. She loves flying through the pretty rings to get to Saturn. She told me last night that Mother Earth is God's wife. She said that the last time she went to visit God, he told her we were all God's children and that no one is any better than any other human being. She claims that everyone's name starts with "Son in Heaven." She told me that soon heaven would be right here on Mother Earth. She said she also wanted to come back to feel different things and learn everything!

Sammy woke up feeling very excited one day. I was feeding her breakfast and she asked if I would scratch her back. She said her wings were itching! She began to explain that they were kind of invisible. She told me she could see mine. I asked her what color her wings were, and she said they were kind of lavender and pink. She went on to say that I could see them if I just closed my eyes and used my third eye. She told me to try it. I did, and as usual, I couldn't see anything. She said, "Concentrate harder." I did, but nothing worked. Then she said, "You need to practice more." She also mentioned that she traveled all night and didn't sleep. I did not probe as to what she saw or where she went.

The Story of Katie
Jennifer Walsh

From the moment Katie was born, I knew that she was not like the others. She possessed an awareness that shocked us. She opened those eyes, and the wisdom of the ages shone forth. When Katie looks at someone, she looks into their soul.

She slept very little. She responded to native chanting but seemed to have a tough time fitting into that little body. She often became very frustrated.

Since I've worked with energy for a number of years, I noticed that Katie was very sensitive to sounds and other people's energy. She was and is especially sensitive to negativity and untruths.

From the time Katie could speak, she told me that she came from a star. Several times I found her gazing at the evening star and chanting to herself.

She has an amazing sense of humor, imagination, and creativity, as well as a great sense of self. Sometimes she would play the game of "creating" with me. She would instruct me to cup my hands and then she would hold her hands around mine. Then all I had to do is create what I wanted.

Katie always knew she was royalty from the beginning, and she accepted nothing less. It's both an honor and a challenge raising this interesting child. We give her choices in almost everything because nothing else works.

This intelligent child soon realized that a lot of the outside world wasn't her world, and she literally stopped talking to everyone with the exception of myself, my husband, our teenage daughter, and a few neighborhood children. She has been labeled a "selective mute," which is an anxiety disorder. She hasn't spoken one word at school in four years. She turned eight in June of 2001.

Katie picks up everyone's energy, and her teachers say she can perceive what they're going to say and do before it happens. One teacher stated that Katie could take charge and run the class if she so chose. She can basically do anything she puts her mind to.

Last summer when her grandmother was dying, I spoke with Katie. She very directly and matter-of-factly told me to tell Grandma not to worry and that she would be just fine. Then, just as casually, she said that Grandma could soon come back as a new baby. She didn't seem to have the need to grieve her passing; it just wasn't an issue. She was upset, however, when she saw Grandmother in the funeral home. She asked why we had to do this when Grandma wasn't there. She needed to understand that others had to say good-bye in the old-energy way.

It's been a painful process to watch this beautiful and gifted child withdraw. Her nature is not quiet, which is difficult for others to believe.

She has some wonderful little friends at school, although she doesn't verbally speak to any of them. These little people often flow around her in a protective circle. Katie and her best friend communicate nonverbally and have a good time.

When Katie begins feeling safer to emerge into her true self, she will slowly progress. When Katie and the others blossom, the world can't help but become a better place!

My helpful hints for parents:

1. Stay in the NOW with your child. Take one day at a time. Don't keep looking down the long road.

2. Love, acceptance, patience, and tolerance are so very important!

3. Understand that this is part of a greater picture. Don't force or apply pressure. The child will only withdraw more.

4. If possible, try not to medicate them. (It nearly destroyed our daughter.)

5. Remember, they're still children. They basically just want to live a fairly "normal" life, for now anyway. They still need us.

Zachary and Tyler
Robin Rowney

I am a single mom of five-year-old twin boys. Both of them, of course, are Indigo kids, and both have many components of the typical diagnosis of ADD and ADHD. I just read *The Indigo Children* in less than two days. I cannot thank you enough for writing such an enlightened piece of work. I devoured the words as quickly as I could.

I want to share two stories about my "angels." The first year of the boys' lives, we all shared the same bedroom in my parents' home (thank God they were there for us). Each boy had his own crib, and I had my bed. They never slept through the night that first year, so I was a very sleep-deprived and depressed mom.

One night after one of my own personal crying sessions, I lay in bed watching the boys sleep. I began to hear Zachary laugh out loud. He laughed so hard that

I thought for sure that my parents would wake up, too. I watched the crib and noticed a very bright golden light hover above him. I was stunned. He quieted down, so I walked over to look more closely. The light faded, and Zack was sound asleep with a huge smile on his face—the smile of a soul who knew all there was to know—a smile of peace. Ironically, this is the boy who rarely sits still and is always on the go.

As for Tyler, he is the "seer." I remember one time when he was about 18 months old and I was slipping him out of his car seat in a mall parking lot. He looked into the car parked next to us, pointed, and said, "Angel." He was seeing an angel in the backseat of the other car. I didn't even know he knew the word *angel*, let alone how to say it! For the next year or so, he'd frequently point out angels, mostly in vehicles. To this day, he frequently dreams of angels—seeing them and being one. What a gift!

I was certainly blessed with two beautiful, priceless gifts. They are my angels.

Thank you again. I will be forever grateful for your book.

We told you that we've received many letters. This one stayed on top of the pile, and we absolutely knew that we wanted to share it with you. It's a story that's hard to put down—about a child's fight for life, and a mother's experience during the struggle. Do miracles happen? Can Indigos perceive what's going on? Can reality change from what the medical profession is used to, to what the Indigo creates? This is a story that will make you celebrate the Indigo Children, and the parents who stand by them.

"Mommy, She's Not Going to Die"
Sally Donovan

On March 18, 1992, I became the proud and rather awestruck mother of an Indigo Child. Of course I didn't know that at the time. I wasn't to hear about the Indigo phenomenon for another six and a half years, but looking back, I realize that all the signs were there.

Within minutes of her birth, my daughter let me know what she wanted her name to be. I had three picked out, and as the hospital personnel laid her on my stomach, I asked her to show me which one she wanted by blinking her wide little newborn eyes, once for yes and twice for no.

"Molly?" Two quick blinks. "Taylor?" Two quick blinks. "Murphy?" One blink.

So Murphy it was. She began speaking late, at two and a half. Well, speaking English anyway. As an infant, she would babble a lot. When she was between 12 and 18 months old, she would unleash a string of what we thought was gibberish, but she was very intent in what she said—with proper cadence and all. I could tell from her eyes that she was trying to tell us something and couldn't figure out why we didn't understand her.

One time when we were driving on the freeway, Murphy pointed to a passing car and said, "That man is bad." Knowing already that she was an old soul, I asked her to tell me more. She went into a long story about what he had done and how sad he was. I could tell that she was frustrated by having such a limited vocabulary with which to tell her story.

Murphy has done that many times since—that is, telling me how "that person over there" feels. Sometimes

I pump her for more information, but she declines. Her interest in them is past already, and she wants to move on to other things.

By the age of three or four, when I would try to explain something to her, Murphy would begin interrupting me adamantly with "I know!" I would ask her how she knew, and she would respond, "Because, Mommy, I know everything!" in a matter-of-fact way. I had no doubts even then that she *did*. Now, when she tells me "I know" or "I just knew it" in a situation, I stop and say, "Oh, yeah, I forgot you know everything." She believes it, and I do, too.

When Murphy was nearly two, we welcomed another little Indigo into our family. Hayley was born on January 6, 1994. She was a quiet baby, not nearly as active as her sister, but her sleeping habits were just as erratic, and many a night I spent with both of them on the couch.

At nine months, Hayley became ill—experiencing frequent vomiting and diarrhea. She went through a barrage of tests over the next six months. At 14 months of age, she still wasn't walking. It was as if she was too weak to stand. No one could find anything wrong until someone suggested she might be gluten intolerant. We removed all wheat from her diet, and her health improved immediately. Two weeks later, she was walking. We kept her on a strict diet, and she was fine.

At Christmastime, right before she turned two, Hayley became sick again. I began another round of doctors and tests. No one could find anything wrong other than an ear infection. Two weeks after her second birthday, it was obvious to me that she was fading away. The night before yet another doctor's appointment, I was crying, sure I was losing her. Murphy was almost four at the time and came up to me and said,

"Mommy, she's not going to die." I felt heartened. Murphy would know the truth.

The next morning, Hayley had a seizure in the doctor's office, and I barely got her to the hospital in time. They told me later in the emergency room that she was "posturing," which is the last thing the body does before the brain dies. The doctors finally told us she had a tumor in her brain the size of a grapefruit. They were prepping her for emergency surgery to remove it. The surgeon said the tumor looked very malignant on the MRI scan and that surgery would be followed by a course of chemo or radiation.

When Hayley was stabilized, we were allowed to see her. I stood at the foot of her bed, and almost as if it were a vision in my mind's eye, a smiling face hovered just above Hayley's still, lifeless form. It was Hayley's face, laughing, and saying, "I'm okay, Mommy. I'm going to be fine, really." I heard this over and over again.

I moved to Hayley's side and took her tiny fingers in my right hand. I placed my left hand on her head. With my eyes closed, I silently called out to the Universe. I asked that all the prayers being said for Hayley be gathered together. I could feel their power as they collected from as far away as London and New Zealand. All at once and with great speed, they formed a band of blinding white light. It came straight for us, like a comet with a glowing tail.

Although my eyes were still closed, I "saw" it come shooting through the hospital window. I felt it enter my body from the right, pass through me down my left arm, out my hand, and right through into Hayley's head. When this band of light hit the tumor, it exploded in a shower of sparks, like fireworks. It was as if the tumor was dis-integrated—obliterated. It was the most beautiful thing

I've ever seen. I was enveloped in a peace I'd never known. There was no doubt in my mind that Hayley was going to fully recover.

After the surgery, the doctor appeared, shaking his head. He said that the tumor didn't appear to be as malignant as he thought, but he wouldn't go so far as to say that it was benign. "*That* would be a miracle," he said.

Well, after having the tissue sample sent to three different labs and even the Mayo Clinic in Rochester, Minnesota, they still couldn't identify it. It was finally classified as a benign tumor, with the only treatment being re-section. It really didn't surprise me. Hayley is truly a miracle child.

Hayley is now a happy, healthy six-year-old. Her gluten intolerance vanished after the surgery, and she has absolutely no diet restrictions. We can see from the latest MRI that her left brain is almost fully regenerated, to the amazement of us all (well, to the doctors, anyway). She was diagnosed with Central Auditory Processing disorder and has been in speech therapy for two years. She is doing wonderfully in kindergarten and is right on target!

I know that angels surround her. At 18 months, she caught her finger in the end of the moving sidewalk at the airport. Within seconds, a man was at our side taking care of her finger, which had been pretty well mangled. While we waited for paramedics, he stayed and administered to her. At the hospital, the doctors were amazed by how well the wound had been taken care of. I looked at the card the man had given me. It said, "Dr. Angelchik!" He truly was an angel to us.

Whenever we have quiet time or meditate together, Hayley will point and say, "There's God," and "There are the angels." She sees them everywhere and even tells me what they're saying to her. I am in awe of that. I wish

I could see what she sees. Once when we were in an airplane flying through the clouds, she pointed and said that God and a bunch of angels were waving to her and saying, "Welcome, Hayley! We're glad you're here."

Many times during upsetting situations, my children will give me the most beautifully simplistic advice. When I'm sad, they offer the sweetest words of comfort. The ideas and wisdom that come out of their mouths is truly a wonder. It stops me in my tracks and helps me realize how out of touch I've become with what is really important.

I was told a year and a half ago by a medium that both my children were "children of the blue ray." I asked around for any information I could on this subject. There wasn't much out there. Then a friend told me about your book, and I knew I had found my answers. I read it without stopping until I got a headache, and then I read some more.

I am now on a crusade to change the way the schools operate. I'm talking to the teachers, parents, and anyone else who will listen. I'm finding that they're very interested and have similar stories to tell me about their children: *They just won't do the work!* I would love to open my own school to provide a nurturing environment for the Indigos to learn in.

Thank you, thank you, thank you for putting your book in print. I now have something I can point to and say, "This is it! These children are special gifts we've been given, and we need to do something about it now! They need our help to change the system to allow them to realize their potential."

Sally indicated that Murphy was able to "see" the fact that Hayley wasn't going to die. Wishful thinking? Or did this Indigo actually see a life force or an interdimensional part of the human being? For that matter, can Indigos see auras? The next story is more than similar—it's really very much the same!

"He's Not Going to Die Today, Is He, Oma?"
Bev Wells

I have an Indigo Child story for you. My-son-in-law, Lloyd, was very ill last Labor Day, and we nearly lost him to an infection in his spine. He'd had an operation on that part of his body, and it had gotten infected. He has three children, and my daughter (his wife) was a wreck, to say the least.

Lloyd needed to have very dangerous surgery done—a shunt placed into his heart so they could inject the antibiotics directly. They were unable to culture the bacteria. It was a new strain; therefore, they didn't know how to treat it. So they treated it with "everything they had."

I brought my three grandchildren to see their father before he went into surgery. He said he wanted to see their faces as the last thing he might see on Earth. I could see his aura, and it looked very dim and almost nonexistent. I was afraid he wouldn't live through the surgery.

I was trying to console my daughter the best I could when they brought Lloyd back out of recovery. The fact that he was still alive was a miracle in itself! My three-year-old granddaughter, Samantha, wanted to come and see her daddy. The other two children were in school, so I took her up to see her dad.

She crawled up on a chair beside the bed and put her face approximately five inches away from her father's face and never moved. Lloyd would open his eyes occasionally and say, "Hi, Sam," and then speak to his wife or to me, then drift off back to sleep.

Finally, my daughter softly said, "Sam, what are you doing?" Samantha turned on the chair, looked her mother in the eyes, and said, "I'm looking at him and listening to him so I will remember him when he's dead." Needless to say, my daughter almost fainted. But then Sam looked at me and said, "But he's not going to die today, is he Oma?" I could see that his aura was much stronger than the day before, and I softly said, "No, Sam, he's not going to die today."

Samantha had seen the aura on the first day, and then she'd been able to see the difference on the second day, but she just didn't know how to describe it. She very casually climbed down off the chair and said, "I didn't think so." Then she asked to go to the gift store to find something for her dad when he woke up. I left my daughter to compose herself and took Samantha to the gift shop, and we got a teddy bear for her dad.

All three of my grandchildren are Indigo Children, but the two girls—Samantha, now four, and Victoria, six, are the most vocal and questioning. My eight-year-old grandson is more reserved, but very interested in the questions his sisters ask.

Victoria asked me whether I had lived before and wondered if I was going to live again. Also, she wanted to know if *she* had lived before and if she was going to live again. Of course I answered her questions truthfully, but since she goes to a parochial school, I suggested that maybe those kinds of questions should be asked of her parents or me and not the teachers at school. She looked at me like only a six-year-old can, and said, "For crying out loud! You don't think I would talk about that at school, do you?"

How stupid of me to doubt.

Auras? Colors around people? Energy? Is it possible that these children can really see these things? Here's the story of an educator who asked the kids to "open up" and let her know.

"Do Any of You See Colors Around Bodies?"
Katherine

My name is Katherine, and a most unusual thing happened to me. Last December I was a substitute teacher working for a small school district in El Monte, California. I was assigned to a first-grade class. There were 20 students in the class, and they were pretty well behaved.

It was the end of the day, and I had brought some of my "energy drawings" just on a whim. (I've been able to draw and color these "energy pictures" with my eyes closed.) I taped them on the front board as the kids were sitting on the rug in front of me. I was sitting in a chair. Something inside told me to ask, "Do any of you see colors around bodies?"

All the students looked at me, then they looked at each other. Then shyly, about five students raised their hands. At that moment, the air became different. I could feel the energy rise, as if a door was opening between me and these kids. It was amazing, incredible, and awesomely beautiful.

One child, who acted a bit immature, grew up right in front of my eyes. His English grammar improved, and he told me he saw a mist of color over people *all the time*. He then identified mine correctly. (I had been informed awhile ago by several people that my aura was gold.) He then identified others: rose, lavender, and pink, and then he pointed out an indigo aura.

This boy, an Indigo Child named Erick, just stared at me, and I stared at him. I then said, "Do you know what we're talking about?" He moved his head up and down very slowly. I then said, "I acknowledge you and am glad to know you." My whole body was tingling all over. I then asked, "Do you know why you're here?" He nodded very slowly. I then said, "You are what we've been waiting for." He nodded. I knew deep down in my heart that this was true.

Other children then told me what they saw. They all knew about auras and angels. I can't remember the first boy's name now, but he told me that he summons spirits. "They come in the form of butterflies made of light. No one else can see them," he said. He travels to other planets with them and is conscious when this happens.

Others told me that they see outlines of color around bodies. They can switch this ability on and off. Other kids see angels on Fridays, and some see angels in January. More incredible things happened that day, but I would have to write a small pamphlet here to cover it. However I will never forget it.

"Grandma, Do You See Angels?"
Barbra Dillenger, Ph.D.

Al is an interdimensional Indigo. He's a large child, nine years of age, and he could easily be mistaken for a young teenager. He has always been a stocky, big-boned, well-developed child. His grandmother, a good friend of mine, calls him the "gentle giant." He is quite philosophical, particularly about the demands of his younger conceptualist sister (*conceptualist* is a kind of Indigo covered in the first book). Al gives in to her easily and without apparent resentment. For the last several years, he's been attending a Catholic elementary school. His grandmother takes care of him and his sister often so that the parents can have some well-deserved alone time.

The family is aware of Grandmother's interest in angels. One night when she was child-sitting, the parents left a present for her. It was a book about angels. The children sat down with her to look at it, but Al was silent.

Later on in the evening, it was homework time. Grandmother, sister, and Al went to the table to complete the task at hand. After a while, out of the blue, Al said, "Grandma, do you ever really see any of the angels, any of your special angels?"

Grandma thought a moment, very carefully choosing her words. "No, honey, I don't ever really *see* my angels. I *feel* them, and I always know when they're there. Sometimes they make me so full of love and joy that I begin to cry."

Al smiled brightly and whispered, "I know, Grandma. I know exactly what you mean." When the homework was finished, Al went to the couch and picked up Grandma's new book. She heard him say, "I feel them, too."

"Mommy, Jesus Will Save Us"
Nikki Dolan

I'd like to contribute something about my daughter, Jessica. Picking an instance is actually quite difficult, since there are many times when her wisdom floors me. I'll give you a few brief examples and let you draw your own conclusions.

I've always been terrified of thunderstorms. Living in "tornado alley" tends to be a rather nervous time for me during the spring and early summer. I've been known to hide in my basement when I hear the first sound of thunder.

In June of 1998, I had been on a mall outing with my husband; my mother; my infant daughter, Emily; and my two-year-old daughter, Jessica. We were driving home, and a very dangerous super-cell with a history of producing tornadoes was rapidly gaining on us. The sky was that ominous green color you hear about and pray you'll never see. True to my nature, I started to panic.

I look back now and see that I was making a complete idiot out of myself in front of my small children. It's a wonder that my fear didn't scar them for life! I panicked for about ten minutes while yelling at my husband to drive faster. Not a word was heard from my daughter until I began to cry from fear. (I know, I'm a wimp.) Suddenly, from the back of the car, a little two-year-old voice stated calmly, "Mommy, Jesus will save us." This was said with the most complete and total faith I had ever heard. I suddenly realized that in my paranoia, I had completely forgotten about my faith in God. I felt like a fool, but also felt enlightened at the same time. The storm soon changed directions and missed us completely. Throughout the entire ordeal, Jessica remained calm, as she always does.

Jessica has an incredible memory. She's almost five years old now and often tells me stories from her life even before she was two. My grandfather died when she was two and a half, and Jessica still remembers going to visit him before he died. She was only in the room for about two or three minutes, but she took all of it in and has been analyzing it ever since.

She often talks about the hospital bed that he was in and the noise from the oxygen machine that was nearby. He died at home, and soon after, they removed the hospital bed from the room he was in. The next time Jessica was at his house, the bed had already been gone for a few months. Jessica only recently asked me if that was his "dying bed" and wanted to know if it went to heaven with him. I don't necessarily find the statement itself amazing. I find the fact that she's still processing information that her brain received almost two and a half years ago, and drawing logical, intelligent conclusions from it quite surprising.

Jessica's favorite phrase is "I love everybody." I firmly believe that she does. She treats everyone that she meets with love and respect and is shocked and deeply wounded when others don't treat her in the same way. She's a very cuddly child, and recently we were having one of our "snuggle sessions" in my rocking chair. I asked her, "Jessica, you have a lot of love inside, don't you?" She said to me, "Of course, Mommy. I was born from love." I had never thought about it that way, but she's so right. She brought tears to my eyes with that statement—tears of pride and joy. She taught me so much, just with that one simple phrase.

My first child died at birth. His name was Douglas, and he was full-term. Jessica was born 13 months after his death. We've always been honest with Jessica about

Douglas. She knows that he died and that he lives in heaven. Oftentimes she will tell me that she's talked to him. She'll give me messages from him. She's told me of her "angel" whose name is Sabrina. I would never tell her she has an overactive imagination (like my parents told me). I truly believe that her experiences with the spirit world are as valid, if not more so, than the experiences we have on this plane of reality.

Remember how we spoke of the way these children sometimes react to profound spiritual things around them? Listen to the tale of David, an eight-year-old. The compassion of these children at early ages is one of the attributes that separates them from the children of the past. Not only do they often relate with compassion and wisdom to those around them, but they also connect at times to the energy of the past.

"I Feel Like Jesus"
Felicitas Baguley

I'm from Berlin, Germany, and I would like to tell you about my eight-year-old son, David. Today I asked him if he would like it if I contributed some of his stories to the authors of a new Indigo book. He said yes, and that he would like to participate. Only one thing came to his mind, however. I asked him what it was. He said, "Well, it's not much, only that I am the follower [successor] of Jesus."

When David was five, he made that statement to me one day. At four or five, he cried bitter tears about Jesus' death. He became really upset emotionally about the fact that Jesus was nailed to the cross. (We talked about that at Easter.) He was crying as if Jesus was a very close relative, being murdered. He said: "I am the follower of Jesus. I feel like Jesus."

There's one other little story when he was about three or four years old: I took him with me to my workplace, which is a kindergarten. It happened that one kid started to provoke him. David simply smiled at the kid very lovingly, and then he turned around.

When I gave birth to David, it was also special. At one point, I had the feeling that I couldn't go on, that there was no energy left to continue giving birth to him. I felt like I would die. I said, "David, please help." Immediately, he slipped out of my body. I also realized that there had been two doctors and two nurses with me giving birth to David. Normally there's just the midwife and a nurse. We—David and I—had some problems with the birth, so help was needed and given.

After David was born, the hospital staff forgot about us long enough to give us the opportunity to stay with each other without disturbance. David watched me in a very intense way for several minutes! (Normally newborns have their eyes closed immediately after birth.) He was constantly looking at *me—into* me. We both looked into each other's eyes—very intensely. Then, back home, of course, we had endless time to share with each other by looking into each other's eyes. Then I could see that David was a *very old, very wise soul.* Much more than I am.

When they're small, no one has yet informed children about doctrinal appropriateness. They don't yet "know" that they're not supposed to relate to Jesus and a past-life experience. The children only feel what they feel, and relate to the love and energy around them.

Some are very clear about who they were before they "got here." Sometimes it's general, and sometimes they give specific names. But often they see "what came before" as something helpful, sometimes as an angel themselves. Again, we say that this compassionate overlay is something that's new. A human being's first years of life are filled with survival energy and primitive emotional learning. Most of us didn't relate to the world around us in a compassionate way until we reached 12 or 13. You have to wonder where the compassion comes from when dealing with these little ones. In the last story, who instructed David in the doctrine of "turning the other cheek"? The answer is that it came naturally from inside him. Not only did he feel like the master of love (Jesus), but he was practicing the words of Christ at four—in kindergarten!

Some would say that since the predominant religion in America is Christianity, kids could pick up on the Christ story very early. After all, Christmas and Easter are filled with it.

But what about an Indian guru?

Remembering Sai Baba
Evelyn Beatty

Hello. I have a story about my Indigo grandson, Quillan.

When he was about 18 months old—just barely walking and talking—he said only a few words—that is, Mama, Nana, Dada, etc. He picked up my book about Sai Baba (a popular and powerful guru residing in India), which had his picture on the cover, smiled, put his fingers and thumbs together to form a triangle, bowed his head, and said, "Sai Baba!"

One day when he was two years old, I was in the bedroom on the phone when I realized that a phone number I needed was in the living room in the rolltop desk. I walked into the living room to get it when I noticed that the paper with the phone number on it was on the chair in front of the desk. Amazed, I asked my daughter, Quillan's mama, how the paper got on the chair. She said that Quillan suddenly got up from where he was playing, opened the rolltop desk, and got the paper out and put it on the chair. He then returned to his blocks!

Quillan is now three years old and draws pictures of people with three eyes. When asked why, he says, "Everybody has a third eye." His mama asked him what you see with the third eye. He replied, "Lots and lots of light—mostly white and silver."

Even though my daughter is very patient, her son can be very challenging—so challenging, in fact, that she got incredibly frustrated one day and found herself glaring at him, hands on her hips, saying, "You're *not* the boss of me." This was to a three-year-old!

Aren't Indigos wonderful? And aren't you both wonderful to have given us all this information?! Our family is very grateful and relieved to know that our precious red-haired boy is normal—and special. Thank you.

Much of our mailbox has been filled with stories of children "remembering" a past experience before this lifetime. Here are some of our favorites.

"Don't You Remember?"
Tracy Cisneros

When my daughter, Misha, was six years old, our family moved to Ecuador. Three months after the move, Misha became severely ill with a high fever and vomiting. I raced her to the hospital emergency room and then realized that it was out of my hands. I had been a nurse for 20 years and knew she needed an IV to hydrate her. She only weighed 32 pounds, and being dehydrated, she felt like a limp rag as I carried her into the hospital.

As she lay on the stretcher, I remembered looking at this sweet little pale face and being so afraid for her life. I explained to her that the nurse was going to put an IV into her arm and how it would only hurt for a moment until the needle was in—then the pain would go away. I told her how she needed to be brave and look at Mama in the eyes to make the fear go away.

This she did, and after the nurse left, I started to explain to my sweet child how I, as a nurse, used to put IVs into children and grown-ups. I explained how I would help them to ease their fears, just like I did with my little girl.

My daughter looked up at me so knowingly in that moment and said, "I know, Mama." I looked at her quizzically and asked how she knew, as I had done this long before she was born.

Her answer so plain and honest: "Don't you remember? I used to watch over you when you were a nurse, from up in heaven with the other angels."

Going to a Higher Level
Yvonne Zollikofer

Yesterday my son, Victor, was playing with some toys in his bathwater, and we began to talk very quietly together.

"Victor, you told me a lot about your lives before coming here. Can you remember anything of the time just before being born here as my child?"

Victor's eyes seem to go far away, and then he replied, "Yes. I had been told to go to Earth to help. On the one hand, I didn't want to come, but on the other hand, I wanted to, so I agreed to come here. So I had to dig a tunnel to come here."

I continued. "Was it dark or light? What did you feel?"

"Oh, very narrow and dark."

"And do you have any idea what will happen when you leave this life?"

"Yeah. The tunnel will be very bright, and I will go to a higher level."

He started to play again, and those are the moments when I stop questioning. . . .

Spiritual Counseling from a Three-Year-Old
Kerry-Lynne D. Findlay Chapman

I wish to tell you about a most profound experience I had with my daughter Donna when she was just three years old. To set the scene, my brother (age 48) had just died of cancer. It was a very trying time for my family.

I have three other brothers, but my only sister, Beverly, died when she was 27, leaving three children—the youngest a newborn. Also, ten years ago, my husband died of a sudden heart attack, and I was a single mom for a while with a son and a daughter. I later married again, and my husband adopted my older two and is the father of my younger two. My husband is younger than I am, but Donna would not have known that at age three.

After my brother's funeral service, back at my mother's home, Donna sat down with me. First it was in the living room, and then later in the bedroom (at her request because it was quieter). There, she told me about heaven. She approached it in such a mature and earnest way that I wrote down notes of what she said and later typed them out. I assume, because of the circumstances surrounding Ron's death, that she felt I was in need of some "spiritual counseling."

Here are the notes from our conversation: Donna Chapman, age 3 years, 9 months, is speaking:

> I want to teach you about heaven. You should learn about it. My father died when he was younger. He was an old man and went to heaven. Then he left heaven and now he is at our house— my father, Brent.
>
> When he was younger, he had a very little story and he died and went to heaven. When he was there, he was not young and not old. Then he came back and he was not an angel anymore.
>
> Let's go somewhere quieter where we can talk. [We went from the dining room to her grandmother's bedroom and closed the door.] I want you to learn about heaven.
>
> You came out first, and then Daddy, and then me, and then Lindsay came back to be with us.

When your son [Beau] was younger, he never came out of the sun because he couldn't fly, and he had to take very bad medicine, like the kind in the hospital.

When I was younger, I was a very old sister, and I never came out of the sun because I was very busy up in the sky.

When you were a baby, I told you about heaven, but you couldn't speak.

Your sister, Auntie Beverly, was too young to leave. She is a little girl now [She told me this twice, that Beverly is now a little girl.]

If you went to heaven, I would be very upset because you're my mommy. But to learn about heaven is a good thing. If you get hurt, you'll have to go to heaven.

A mom's reflection on this:

Note the mature way (at three) that she spoke to me with authority and self-confidence. She first speaks of her father, Brent, and that he has lived before. She refers to him having a short life before, and how he's in heaven where we are neither young nor old. She speaks of him being an angel after he died. She mentions that I "came out first," then her daddy, then herself, and then Lindsay—which is the correct birth order. She mentions Lindsay (the youngest) "coming back to be with us." She talks about herself being "very busy up in the sky." She tells me that my sister, Beverly (now deceased), is back on Earth as a little girl.

"The Best Mom I Could Have Chosen"
Angela Graves

I'm unsure if my little boy is an Indigo Child, but he fits the characteristics. From the time he was an infant, he slept very little and was very alert—so much so that when he was with me during my doctor's visit at about two months old, my doctor took out his light and shined it around the air in front of him from about four feet away. The doctor commented on how Alex's eyes followed the light with every movement. He said that it was unusual for a baby to be that alert at his age, and told me he would probably be very bright.

Alex was talking in sentences very early. He knew his colors at one and a half, sang full songs from cartoons with arm gestures, vibrato, in character at three, and started having problems in preschool at that time, also.

He had trouble socializing. He wanted to play with the older five-year-olds who excluded him, and he was determined to join them. He is not meek by any means. He is one of the most challenging people I have ever been in the company of. His energy is exhausting, and he will push every button that you have. I had his IQ tested at four because of his behavior—to see if there was anything wrong before we entered him in school. Even the grandparents had mentioned his hyperactivity. We found his IQ to be 156—way above average, to the point that it's hard for him to fit in.

He told me that I am the best mom he could have chosen. I asked what he meant by that, and he said, "Before I was in your tummy when I was still with God, I looked all over the world and chose you to be my mommy and Dad to be my daddy out of everyone else because I thought you would be the best mommy and daddy for me, and I was right—you are."

He also used to tell me he was scared to sleep alone because there was a man (a spirit) who would come into his room if I was not there. This lasted for three years. It finally stopped when I told him that he could ask the man to leave or ask God to make him leave. He also used to talk to me about his brother, Jerry (he has no brother Jerry).

We were sitting in the truck one day when he said, "Mom, do you remember when Jerry took my hot dog and ate it all up and didn't leave me any?"

I said, "No, who's Jerry?"

"You know. My brother, Jerry."

"You mean your brother, Ben?"

"No, my other brother, Jerry."

"You don't have another brother."

"You know, my other brother with my other mother before you and Ben," he said.

He doesn't remember it anymore, but he talked about it until he was about four.

Butter in His Tea?
Anna

The first odd thing regarding my son was that the pregnancy test (done properly) did not show I was pregnant a month after my evident conception of my child, Samuel (born in July 1995).

Samuel learned to walk and talk fairly late (around his second birthday), but since the age of one, he has seemed to understand speech very well. At the age of three, Samuel started to use abstract terms and concepts such as "my thoughts, my imagination, happiness, badness." He was capable of role-playing (psychologically) at some level even at this young age. He has an awareness of his own inner world being separate from the material world, as well as the points of view of other people. He also uses words such as *man* and *people* in a peculiarly objective way, almost like an outsider at times.

Samuel is an energetic, talkative boy, mainly interested in things normal to a four-year-old (like toy cars and computer games). Yet on an everyday level, he asks intelligent questions such as, "Why are Indians called Indians even though they don't live in India? Are people animals or not? How cold does it have to be for water to turn into ice?"

Samuel often brings up moral issues concerning right and wrong. It has been self-evident for him that there are different nations speaking different languages in this world. He sometimes inquires of me what this or that is called in English or French. Samuel seems to know some customs of other cultures of which he has not been informed. He, for example, demanded butter to be put in his tea because "that is the way they drink tea in China."

What follows is a story from Bea Wragee. She is a teacher, healer, and energy worker. She taught middle school in Michigan before moving to California. There she spent some years in the publishing industry before devoting her time to her work in metaphysics and to raising her son. Using loving energy, she creates flower essences for people and animals. With her husband, she also does energy healing in homes and businesses. She has created a special Indigo Essence to help these special children deal with their journey on this earth. You can contact her at: **beabobeth@aol.com**.

My Journey Through Motherhood —Raising an Indigo Healer
Bea Wragee

When my son was ten months old, Frank Alper, a gifted mystic and teacher, told me that he had to talk to me about my son. Now I had just walked into the room and was taken back by his directness. He went on to tell me that my son was a soul of the highest magnitude and that he was here on this planet to help heal mankind. It was the most important part of my service to protect him from the harshness of the world. Quaking with the responsibility of this information, I asked, "How do I do that?" He replied, "Remember what was done to you, and do the opposite."

Perhaps I should go back to the beginning. On my 40th birthday, I received the results of my amniocentesis and was also told that everything was fine and that I was going to have a boy. I was delirious. When I went into labor and all through delivery, I felt no pain. I was in harmony with this tiny soul entrusted to me and my husband. When Trey was born, he was full of light. His eyes were riveting and magnetic. People I didn't even know in the hospital stopped and commented. I guess that right then we knew he was special.

There are many examples of how this Indigo Child expressed his unique abilities and gifts. I will include a few just to give you an idea of the dynamics of our family. Trey is a *humanitarian* Indigo who from time to time also takes on the characteristics of an *artistic* Indigo. He is a gentle soul who uses a refined approach rather than an aggressive one to get his needs met.

When he was barely four, our car broke down on the freeway during rush-hour traffic. Now in California, that's a major challenge. As we sat on the side of the road in the dark with cars whizzing by, I asked, "What are we going to do now?" Trey looked at me with those huge eyes of his and said, "Don't worry, Mommy. We'll just use our love power and make someone stop." The words weren't even out of his mouth when a truck stopped to help. The man told me that he never, ever stops on the freeway, but he looked at my son and had to stop. Not only did he check the car, but he also drove us all the way home.

Once, on vacation, my husband was quite ill. Trey told me that we needed to do some healing on Daddy. I agreed. He told me that I should take the stomach, and he would take the head and knee. When I had finished my work, I asked Trey how he did his energy work. He explained that he pictured Jim as if he were in a video game and then sent his energy out to the parts of his body that were sick. Remembering Frank's words, I told Trey that I thought it was a great way of doing the work. I can't imagine exactly what kind of response my mother would have given, but I know she would not have believed me. Oh, by the way, Jim felt much, much better in the morning.

School issues have caused some challenges, but surprisingly, we seem to be weathering them quite well. In the early years, Trey went to a Montessori school. Then, for some life lessons of his own, Trey was pressed to go to public school. I worried and fretted at first, but I finally saw that for him, it was important to understand how all of the children experienced school. The thing that I'm clear about is that I trust in his perceptions of his experiences. If he expresses some doubt about school, I start with his observations and explanations. There is no "What did you do to make this happen" in the conversation.

Now that Trey's in high school, there are even more challenges relating to the value of homework, certain lessons, and the importance of speaking your truth. This is not always an easy task in a system that requires compliance with the "norm," but as I said, Trey has a quick mind and a smooth delivery. In his gentle way, he has been able to question teachers and to speak his truth to them without creating too much chaos. In that, we're lucky.

One day when he was in the seventh grade, Trey announced to me that he could tell where people were even when he couldn't see them. I asked him how he did it. He told me that he just sent his energy out of his heart, and it would reach out to another person and he could tell where they were. "It works sort of like sonar," he said. I was impressed with his candor and also with his ability to translate the process into an understandable explanation. He told me with a little consternation that he couldn't do it with everyone—just the people he liked.

I am now 16 years into my first adventure as a mother. I know that God in his infinite wisdom waited for me to develop a greater sense of self and more awareness of the spiritual connection that I've always had before allowing this delightful soul to come to me. I believe that whatever choices my son makes in his life, he knows that he is loved, respected, and trusted. I learned very early to speak truthfully to him no matter how much discomfort it might have brought me. My reward is that he loves and trusts me in return. What a wonderful gift!

We received a letter from a grateful teacher, Mary Ann Gildroy, who appreciated the Indigo information and who said she has witnessed the Indigo phenomenon herself over the 24 years that she has been an educator. Her comments to us were that the Indigo books are mostly for parents, and that educators need to have a "how-to" book, too. She went on to give us sound reasons why some of the schools seem to be failing, saying that there's army of teachers who could raise the level of their expertise if they only had some practical, affordable assistance in their classrooms.

We agree. Perhaps that will be the subject of the next Indigo book—a guide for teaching the Indigo Child. If it is, then we will honor Mary Ann in its pages!

For now, we wish to honor this educator by publishing her poem. It's a message from a teacher to her children, and we are proud to include it here. It's dedicated to all the educators who can hardly wait to get the general public on-board to support them—a group of teachers who can shape up an older system to allow for a new consciousness of student . . . called the Indigo.

I Take You Home
Mary Ann Gildroy

I take you home with me in my head every night.

You are the reason my eyes won't shut and the thoughts come racing.

I see your face—sometimes full of sun, lit with trust and expectation.

I see your face—sometimes closed by self-doubt and the lonely unsureness that is part of growing up.

You are my inspiration, my frustration, my greatest challenge, and above all, my greatest gift.

Reflected in your eyes I see who I am.

You are my student.

I take you home with me in my heart every night.

You are the reason my eyes won't shut and the thoughts come racing.

(© 1994, used with permission)

Well, this is the spiritual chapter, and we've given you stories from children who related to everything from Jesus and Sai Baba to past lives. Now it's time to hear from one of our favorite Jewish scholars. Rabbi Wayne Dosick, Ph.D., is an educator, writer, spiritual guide, and healer who teaches and counsels about faith, spirit, and ethical values. He is the author of six books, and a man who loves children. His words were written just after the school shooting in Santee, California, in March of 2001.

Rabbinic Insights
Rabbi Wayne Dosick

Again.
Again, the bullets rang out at two schools.
Again, innocent children lay dead and wounded.
Again, teenagers are the brutal perpetrators.
Again, we are in great, great pain.
Again, we say, "Enough!"
But, saying "enough" is no longer enough.
We need real answers. We need real solutions.

Here's the problem. Everyone who works with our children—all the educators, and all the doctors, and all the therapists and counselors, and all the mental health professionals, and all the authors, and all the government programs, and all the social service agencies, and all the parents—have tried to heal our children. And, to some extent, everyone has succeeded. But, collectively, we have all failed.

We have failed not only our children who have no conscience and bring guns to school, but also our children who do not know the difference between right and wrong, and also our children who "don't fit in," and "don't get along," and "act out." We have failed our children who we put in "special education classes," and, when all else fails, we medicate with drugs. We have failed our children who live lives of fantasy, who spend countless hours playing video games and surfing the Net.

We have failed, because we all try to heal our children on a cognitive, intellectual, rational level.

But, our children's woundings are on an energetic, spiritual level. And that is where our children must be healed.

Here is what I believe:

Our children are born into this world as pure light channels of God. They are filled with God's light and love. Their old, old souls are still "warm" with the memory of eternal and universal knowledge. They hold a knowing and a vision of a world of joyful and harmonious perfection.

They come in perfection, and they are tossed into our wildly imperfect world. On the "inside," they intuitively know what is right and good. On the "outside," they experience all that is wrong and evil with our world.

When they feel this great chasm between the perfection and holiness of their source, and the bruised and battered existence they find here, their hearts and their souls ache. They are deeply pained by the great dissonance they feel between the perfection they inherently know, and what they encounter in the imperfection of Earth-experience.

They become like shattered vessels, unable to hold the light, unable to sustain holy God-energy.

Many others experience emotional woundings here on Earth. As much as we want to care for them and protect them, our children can never be shielded from the slights wittingly or unwittingly given, real and imagined—of everyday life.

For most adults, life's greatest pain and loneliness comes when, through our own actions or our own thoughts, we somehow disconnect and are separated from God. For our children, life's greatest pain, angst, and existential loneliness comes because, even though they desperately want to stay connected to God, the discordant forces of Earth-life cause shattering and bring about separation.

While these, our children, are often described as "extremely bright . . . precocious," and "wise beyond their years," they are often seen as unhappy, angry, and depressed. They are termed difficult children who have trouble at home and at school. Sometimes they are diagnosed as learning disabled, hyperactive, or attention-deficient.

Our precious children—God's gift to ever-expanding world consciousness—deserve to be healed from their pain and affirm for themselves—and us—the Oneness of the universal soul. They need to teach us that real enlightenment is the knowing that there is never really any separation; there is only Oneness with God and with the universe.

So, how do we heal our children?

To transform negative behavior, we have to get to the source of the behavior. And the source of our children's negative behavior is on the energetic, spiritual level, where they are wounded.

So, picture this: If we drain water from a car battery, the car cannot move, because its power source is drained of its charge.

In the same way, if we can "drain the energy" from a child's emotional wounding, it no longer has the power charge. Then, the wound has no energy. The child can heal. The negative behavior stops. The flow of light and love is open.

We have identified 17 emotional woundings that a child can experience: anger, grief, fear, distrust, despair, anguish, shame, insecurity, selfishness, loss, panic, inferiority, hatred, indignation, resentment, jealousy, and guilt. Each one of these wounds can be present not only in the emotional body, but can reside in a specific place in the physical body as well, causing physical pain.

The way to "drain the energy" from each of the spiritual woundings is to do a little ritual—to play a little game—designed to heal that particular wounding.

We call these games "YOUMEES," because they're done between "you" and "me," the parent and the child. On the surface, it may seem as if these games have little to do with a particular wound or behavior, but the healing is being done at an energetic, spiritual level. It is there that the YOUMEES work. Each YOUMEE can be played in two or three minutes; an entire YOUMEE session takes no more than an hour and a half.

The parent is not the healer, nor does the parent impose a healing on a child. Rather, the parent is the facilitator—a caring, loving helper—for the healing and transformation that comes from the spirit and energy of God, and the universe that embraces—and is embraced by—the child's soul. Spiritual healing is swift. How do we know?

We've conducted a little research project, testing a small sample of children who have played the YOUMEES with their parents. Parents report significant changes in children's behavior and attitudes as soon as one to four weeks after playing the YOUMEES.

Skeptics may call this "California woo-woo," but it is very, very real. For now, we know where our children's pain originates; we know were it resides; we know the holy place—the deepest of the deep on the inside of the inside—where we must go to facilitate healing. And we know what is at stake.

For only when our children's emotional wounds are healed can our world move to a higher dimension, to a higher soul—vibrational—level.

Moving to that higher dimension will mean that we will all have greater wisdom and understanding; that we can know beyond knowing and see beyond seeing, that our senses will be keener, that our consciousness will be more highly evolved, that we will all be more fully immersed in God-energy and more reflective of God-light.

Then, and only then, can our world move beyond the limitations of the present into a time and place where universal healing can take place, where the ancient hope and promise of a perfect world can become reality. "The little children will lead them."

When we heal our children's emotional woundings where they reside on the energetic, spiritual level, our children can be healed from their pain. They can be healthy and whole.

Then we can say, "Never again!" Never again should we have to witness our children playing out their pain with aberrant behavior, their anguish with schoolyard guns.

Then our children can lead us toward the perfect world they know and envision.

If you'd like to talk more about healing our children, or if you'd like more information about what I've discussed here, please call: (760) 943-8577, or toll-free: (877) SOUL KID.

(Originally published in the *San Diego Jewish Times*.)

"*To rescue our children we will have to let them save us from the power we embody: we will have to trust the very difference that they forever personify. And we will have to allow them the choice, without fear of death: that they may come and do likewise or that they may come and that we will follow them, that a little child will lead us back to the child we will always be, vulnerable and wanting and hurting for love and for beauty.*"

— *June Jordan,* U.S. poet and civil rights activist[1]

The Older Indigos

During our metaphysical seminars throughout the world, the Indigos have always been a hot topic. It made us realize that *The Indigo Children* had been released in a very timely manner, and many parents and educators related to it.

What we didn't expect, however, was something that became very obvious around the second month after publication of the book. It seemed that a number of older people felt that they also had been Indigos!

We have to put this into perspective. *The Indigo Children* included a story about recent human evolution (or so we believe). The pioneer in the field, Nancy Tappe, started "seeing" the Indigo color within children before she published her book *Understanding Your Life Through Color,*[5] in 1982. She really can't recall the first time she saw the Indigo color, but she feels that there are probably no pure Indigo humans over the age of 36.

In the first book, we mentioned that many "older" Indigos (in their 20s and 30s) had probably had a rough time of it, and we presented two stories from Indigos that confirmed that fact. We also indicated that, like most other things that evolve over time, the Indigos had probably been arriving slowly for many years. It was only now that we're noticing the differences, and dealing with a new paradigm of parenting and educating. This explains why the first Indigo book was such a revelation.

Suddenly, however, we're facing something else—and in a very focused sector (that of metaphysical and spiritual workers). Many who are in their 40s and 50s feel that they meet all the Indigo criteria! Could it be that they were forerunners of the Indigos? Or maybe they weren't true Indigos at all, but simply possessed some of the Indigo attributes.

Before we delve into that conundrum, here is a sampling of some of the letters and messages we received on the subject.

Pre-Indigos
Nan Sunshine

Would it be possible to start this *new* book with just a few brief passionate words about pre-Indigo people in biology!

There are sooooo many people who need to be honored and given a standing ovation for their steadfast "holding of the light" that got us to this point in time where the word *Indigo* even exists.

For many generations, there have been handfuls of people here and there who have stood strong for change. There were many times where this "single voice" was all alone, pleading for new forms of thinking and being. They were the ones rising up to the Universe with proclamations that "we can be more." They were the ones who came through with a greater love than that which commonly existed. They were the ones who were the "stormy rebels" and went against the grain of society.

They may have at times looked liked the fools, but today they are truly the pre-Indigos who paved a new paradigm that shook the very foundation of humanity's fiber. Because of these people, we now truly stand on the threshold of a greater expansion of being.

Who are these people? They are the ones who are reading this, and they also represent many people who have since passed. Perhaps they're standing over our shoulders as we write this, saying, "If we could do it all over again, we would." Smiling and winking, they would say, "We pulled it off. So be it!"

Pre-Indigos? Nan just named it. These may be forerunners of the Indigo Children who believe that they were Indigos, or at least the beginning of the wave that we're seeing now. Here are four more letters. They ask the same question in various ways, the first one even offering a logical explanation. We realized that we had opened an entire new subject of discussion.

Life Is Process
Umar Sharif, M.A.

Thank you so much for your book regarding the Indigo Children. As an educator and consultant, I spend a lot of time advocating for a new way of nurturing, educating, and understanding our children. I, and others in my circle, have been noticing the phenomenon of what I have referred to as "The Gathering" for some time. I am also a father of five children, my youngest (Ashanti) now

12 years old. Some of my most rewarding spiritual conversations have been in my talks with him since he was about three or four years old. I certainly wish that I had been wiser in raising my oldest son (Mansur), who I believe is a very wounded Indigo—a very bright and articulate 25-year-old who dropped out of high school, didn't get his General Education degree, but who is a self-taught computer whiz.

I have, what is for me, a very important question. Natural phenomena do not generally occur in sharp linear breaks. Life is process. Your book and the authors cited seem to place the Indigo Child phenomenon from the '70s on. Is it possible that Indigo Children began coming into the world decades earlier, but in such few numbers that they went from birth to adulthood without being noticed?

My question is based on two observations. First, Olodumare (God) always sends Ogun (the defender of the way) to clear the way for His/Her emissaries or His/Her purpose. If some 90 percent of humans being born in recent decades are Indigos, my guidance tells me that there had to be a vanguard being born decades earlier. A vanguard to *see*, *say*, and *save*.

Second, I'm only on page 43 of your book, but I would affirm that you and your contributing authors are talking about me, my childhood, my worldview, and my characteristics. But I'm 53 years old! (born in 1947).

Learning and Evolving
Jaye Powers

Regarding Indigos and their stories, I have two children, now in their teens, who certainly fit the descriptions. But I have another question for you: The descriptions also seem to fit *me!* Are there older Indigo types? I am a 44-year-old female and feel embarrassed asking this, but boy, can I relate to the Indigo experiences!

My children are very advanced, intelligent, sensitive, perceptive, and "feel different" from many of their peers. Raising them has fit well with me because I understand so much of their feelings and experiences.

It seemed pretty understandable and natural to me that I would have children like this. I hadn't heard of Indigo Children before just recently reading this book, but I not only recognized my children (ages 13 and 15), but myself as well.

Have you heard of this? Older Indigos? Any light you might be able to share with me on this would be greatly appreciated. I, like others, still struggle with being "different," and my children have been a great blessing to me. I have a deep faith and continue to learn and evolve.

A New Understanding
Barbara Brandt

I happened to read an article about your book, *The Indigo Children.* I had never heard of this before, but as I read your descriptions of the children, waves of recognition and realization flooded over me. I am 56 years old. I fit all the criteria you described!

From my first glimmerings of self-consciousness (when I was about four or five years old), I always knew exactly who I was. By five, I had decided what I was going to do in the world—bring about healing and social change to affect large numbers of people.

I always knew I was part of God, and I couldn't understand why people who claimed to be religious acted so awfully. Even at the age of five, if my parents used harmful discipline on me, I wouldn't be angry so much as astounded that they didn't know any better! That's not how you help a child learn.

I suffered plenty because I saw the misery that other people were causing themselves, but they didn't understand what I knew, so I realized I had to hide and protect myself until a time when I would be able to "flower."

I was lonely for most of my life because I didn't know anyone else like me, but mostly I longed for someone to explain the contradictions in my life. I knew I was okay, and the world couldn't be bad—something just wasn't working yet.

Have you heard this from any others who are my age?

"I'm Here As a Teacher"
Mike Meloy

I've just finished reading your book. Thank you. After reading the book, I find that the descriptions and stories relate to my own life!

I was born in 1964, so I'm thinking that we started arriving earlier than the '80s. I understand that you're classifying in general groups, and in a lot of ways I fit into the humanist division. However, I think I more appropriately fit into your interdimensional classification.

As early as the age of eight, I was playing counselor to my family and friends. As I got older, I found that complete strangers would tell me their entire life stories. I would listen to them and would offer them advice about how to handle everyday situations that, as an eight-year-old, I would not have known how to handle. I am now 35 and find that I'm still operating as a counselor and a guide.

I've always known that I'm here as a teacher, love being the key. This book describes my experiences in entirely too much detail. I was sure that there were others, but hadn't yet met them. I would love to sit and discuss all of this with someone.

One of Nancy Tappe's students, Barbara Bowers, wrote a book in 1989 called *What Color Is Your Aura?* Some, like Joyce Tutty below, have written us, saying that Barbara also knew of the colors and confirmed what Nancy had introduced. Some didn't even know about Nancy's book and referenced Barbara's book in their messages. Barbara Bowers is no longer with us, but we wish to honor her work as well.

"I'm Normal and Acceptable"
Joyce Tutty

I'm a 45-year-old Canadian Indigo female who has never even met another Indigo Child or vice versa! First Barbara's book, and now yours, has overwhelmed me emotionally—to read about myself as a normal, acceptable person, not someone who is inherently faulty by most everyone else's standards. I always knew who I was, but to know that others know and understand what I'm like and that so many more are being born is wonderful.

Both you and Barbara indicated that the Indigos are at least a generation after mine. Do you know of any other Indigos who are in their 40s or older? I would love to be able to communicate with one of them. To interact with someone of like mind seems too impossible to imagine after spending so many years alone not encountering any!

Before we give you more to think about, you should know that we return to Nancy Tappe in the next chapter, and we asked her this exact question: *Could there be older Indigos— precursors of what we're seeing now?* When you read her answer, you'll understand that the Indigos, although a new "color," are a mixture of many who came before. Nancy tells us that many who "feel" like Indigos were therefore very much vanguards—but not Indigos.

So perhaps these older Indigos were not a "pure Indigo" color. They didn't have all the Indigo energy that would allow them to be "seen" as Indigo. As Umar Sharif said (earlier), perhaps these were emissaries of a type of human to come. This is truly a speculative question, and one that we cannot answer. However, we can still report that the questions do not stop relating to this subject, and many who are older continue to "recognize" themselves in the Indigo paradigm. Therefore, we want to present something else regarding it.

Many who write us also give us information that we feel is a "wink" from the Universe. They tell us that because they had an "Indigo-type" childhood, they stewarded their own Indigo Children in a way that was unique to parenting. Jaye Powers (above) said this: "Raising them has fit well with me because I understand so much of their feelings and experiences."

What if some of these forerunners were here to allow the pure Indigos to grow up with a better chance of understanding themselves? Could such a thing be? This is, of course, a spiritual question. In much of the mail we've received, some of which we have shared with you, there have been stories from older parents and also teachers who claim that their experiences as forerunners enabled them to fulfill their passion—that of raising or teaching others just like them! They knew how the Indigos thought, and what they would do next. They understood how to "get through," and how to succeed where others were having difficulty.

God has filled our world with appropriateness, as well as these kinds of wonderful synchronicities (which we teach about in our seminars). We also tell people that they all have the ability to move their lives in any direction they wish—that sometimes the rut they're in looks inescapable but that it's really an illusion. We have the ability as humans to lift up humanity or destroy the things around us. It's all about free choice, you know.

If Indigos chose their parents (as reported from the children in some of our previous stories), then how appropriate it is that they might have chosen the forerunners! Accidental, or by design? We suppose that only the children know that—and keep it to themselves in those first months of life—without language to let them say, "Hi! I know who you are!"

Here are some examples of forerunners who wrote us. The first one is a reply to the story about Ryan Maluski, which can be found in the last chapter of the Indigo Children book (page 201). Ryan related what it was like to be an Indigo in his 20s (at that time). You might enjoy this reply, addressed to Ryan.

Dear Ryan:

I just finished reading your story in the Indigo book and felt completely compelled to immediately write to you. I am also an Indigo Child and have been painfully aware of my differences from others from a very early age. There are so many elements and similarities in your life story that are like mine. I just feel in some way distressed that I did not know you when you were going through these trials of misunderstanding, because I would have been a person who would have said, "I completely understand, and can relate to what you are experiencing."

The only thing that I see glaringly different about our stories is that I was born in 1951, not in the '70s and '80s. Because of the oppressive attitudes at that time, in society in general and in my parents in particular, I withdrew within myself to protect my private life with God and the spiritual realm. It was the only way to survive. I was intimidated about telling my story to my parents, other adults, teachers, or ministers, because I experienced and sensed their imminent mockery.

I am now the mother of three Indigo children and am successfully raising them to be outstanding people, not because of the Indigo book, but because I intuitively understood that they were different, like me. They required tremendous devotion and care on my part as a parent— very different from the way my parents treated me.

I gained practical wisdom and the working insight necessary to raise these children into marvelous human beings who are now receiving honors on a regular basis. I've been employing the suggestions made in the book for 15 years.

I feel so excited! I just want to tell everybody I know who is an Indigo Child to read this book and feel affirmed and relieved!

— *Vanessa*

Dear Jan and Lee:
I just wanted to thank you for finding the other Indigos and me. I am a 41-year-old yoga teacher in California. I have an M.A. in spiritual psychology and teach children. My business is called *Indigo Yoga,* and I have developed a yoga program for children of all ages that incorporates yoga *asanas* (postures), breathing techniques, imagination games, affirmations, visualizations, and so on.

I read your book with much amazement as I noted each characteristic of the Indigo and recognized myself. I have always felt a little too "before my time." Anyway, I just wanted to thank you and say hello. I'm happy to send you information on Indigo Yoga and my upcoming teachers' training for yoga teachers and parents on how to work with their children.

— *Pamela Hollander*, **Indigo Yoga for Children of All Ages, 1830 Avenida Mimosa, Encinitas, CA 92024**

Yoga for Indigo Children? Yes. Here's a quote from a full-page article in *Time* magazine (February 19, 2001) called "Om a Little Teapot," by Ñadya Labi.

"For stressed-out kids, yoga offers the road to inner peace. For their parents, any sort of peace is nice."

The writer goes on to speak of a national organization in Michigan City, Indiana, called *YogaKids*, which certifies adults to teach yoga to kids and will graduate at least 35 teachers this year.

We've also been informed of Indigo summer camps and work groups for kids. We bet that many of them are organized and taught by the forerunners of the Indigo color—perhaps not pure Indigos, but enough so that the children can relate, and feel safe with a grown-up.

"For success in training children,
the first condition is to become as a child oneself,
but this means no assumed childishness,
no condescending baby-talk that the child
immediately sees through and deeply abhors.
What it does mean is to be as entirely and simply taken up
with the child as the child himself is absorbed by his life."

— ***Ellen Key***, Swedish author[1]

chapter four

Our Second Interview with Nancy Tappe

In our first Indigo Children book, we introduced Nancy Ann Tappe. Nancy is the woman who first mentioned the Indigo Children in her 1982 book called *Understanding Your Life Through Color*.[5] This was the first known publication where the behavior patterns of these new children were identified. Nancy classified certain kinds of human behavior into color groups, and intuitively created a system that is startlingly accurate and revealing. This metaphysical book is fun to read, and you can't help but identify your own traits somewhere in her system (while laughing at yourself), and marvel at how accurate it seems to be.

It has now been two years since the research and publication of *The Indigo Children,* and we wanted to return to Nancy and ask her additional questions. As stated in the first book, Nancy noticed very early on, when she was working on her Ph.D., that there was another color starting to be "seen" in newborns. It started to show itself in the '70s, and she labeled it in her publication in the '80s.

To really gain the most from the following question-and-answer session, it would be helpful for you to read the three interviews with Nancy that appear in the first Indigo book. You can find them starting on pages 6, 47, and 126.

This material discusses the *types* of Indigos: *humanist*, *conceptual*, *artist*, and *interdimensional*. You might also be interested in a newspaper interview related to the Indigos and Nancy Tappe that's published on the Internet at **www.kryon.com/jantober/j_indigo.html**. This will give you additional information to help you understand this chapter.

Remember as you read the following that Nancy regards this subject as "high science," and she teaches about these personal identity colors worldwide. Not everything you read here is understandable immediately, but her book greatly helps to unscramble some of what she refers to. The colors you may hear Nancy describe (the violets, blues, greens, yellows, and the tans) all have specific character attributes that are explained in her book.

Another Private Session with Nancy Ann Tappe
Interview by Jan Tober

JAN: Before we talk about the children, we want to pose a question that many parents are asking: Many who are in their 40s and 50s feel that they meet all the Indigo criteria. Could it be that they are the forerunners to the Indigos?

NANCY: These people are violet. There are many degrees in the colors. Everybody is not the same age spiritually. Do you understand? Some have been doing it much longer than others, and some in a different way than others, and it's like going to a university. We choose different fields and different interests. For instance, we may all be taking political science, but within that broad topic, there is law, health, psychology—there are different roles in that political science that require us to learn differently and do different things.

JAN: Are you saying that some violets are different *tones* of violet?

NANCY: Yes, according to what their program is. I've always said this: A violet born in an affluent home will act differently from a violet born in the ghetto. A violet born in an academic household will be different from a violet born in a nonacademic home. A violet born in an artistic environment will be different from a violet born in the mines of West Virginia.

JAN: Sure, but how would their hues be different?

NANCY: It's not the hue or shade; it's the matrix within it. Now, most of the time I don't put that out in a public statement or in a private reading simply because it would take too long to define it and be too confusing to the general public.

JAN: Is this something you can define for us now?

NANCY: I can define it, but it's a matter of how they operate. I think there are violets there. As I keep saying, the *humanist* types are replacing the yellow and the violet. Therefore, their persona is going to have many attributes of the yellow and the violet within it. Those are the "people violets" that just charm the daylights out of folks. Then there is the Indigo *conceptual* who's replacing the tan and the green within the violet. Then the Indigo *artist* is replacing the blue within the violet. And the Indigo *interdimensional* is replacing the violet.

Now, the violet that's in the *interdimensionals* represents the weird ones, and they can be in every field, but they do things that are abstract. They will bring in new philosophies and new religions. Lee [speaking of the co-author of this book] would fit into that category. You see what I'm saying? He's a violet. He would also fit in as a *conceptual* because he's tan. Do you see what I'm saying on that level? So he's not only abstract and doing something that some people might not understand, but he also tries to be very logical, which is the tan.

JAN: Yes.

NANCY: He doesn't have the yellow. You have that. He also doesn't have the blue, the *artist*. You have that. So one of the things that makes you two a good working team is that you have the *humanist* and the *artist* traits. He has the *conceptual* and the *interdimensional* processes. But he's not an Indigo, and neither are you.

JAN: And the people who feel they're Indigos—do they have the same traits as Indigos or not?

NANCY: They have the same *consciousness* as the Indigo.

JAN: So they can carry some of the similar traits?

NANCY: They will have some of the similar traits, but more important, the Indigos have *their* traits. Do you see what I'm saying?

JAN: The Indigos have the traits of the other colors?

NANCY: Yes, and more. That's what we have to remember. It's not just the violets who feel like they might be pre-Indigos. It's the violets, the blues, the greens, the yellows, and the tans. All of those colors have a process that is part of the Indigo Child. You see, what we're doing is coming down to a one-mindedness. In the Book of Revelations, it's referred to a lot of times as the "four corners" and the "four angels holding the four winds," saying, "Do not let the wind blow until this time has passed." You see?

I look at that like the four types of Indigos. How I have been defining it is that we have the third dimension and the fourth dimension. Right now, we're right about here [Nancy marks on a board], closer to the edge. So the

Indigos, so far, even though they haven't really stepped off the cliff yet, have built part of the bridge. That has been with the assistance of the violets. And the violets will be supervising it, but they've got to build this bridge across here [Nancy marks again]. This will take 200 to 400 years, depending on how fast we learn and grow. We *could* do it in 200 years, but it may take 400, at which time these bodies will no longer have an immune system. There will be changes. This body will not look like it looks today nor perform like it performs today, but the violets are the first start of that. The rest of us will follow.

JAN: What is taking over for the immune system?

NANCY: The endocrine system. So, depending on how fast the Indigos can build that bridge, we, you, me, and Lee may come back to spur that on. But the Indigos who are under 20 now do not even want to look at the past. They do not want to follow our rules. They know their rules are going to be different. The ones now have a mixture of the past and the future. Some of them are rebelling against the past; some of them are accepting it and trying to move on. For the next six years, they'll be going through tremendous changes because, as I say, they'll be getting their rules in kind of a "drip feeding," one drop at a time. So it's not going to be an overnight sensation. It will gradually set in, and we'll suddenly realize that there's somebody else running the world other than the violets. So that's the key that we want to try to get across to the violets: They do have some of that information, but not more than a teaspoonful. What we somehow have to get across to them is that they're perfectly all right as violets; they're not deficient because they're violets.

JAN: We had a letter that stated: "Natural phenomena do not generally occur in sharp linear breaks. Life is process.

Your book and the authors cited seem to place the Indigo Child phenomenon from the '70s on. Is it possible that Indigo Children began coming into the world decades earlier, but in such few numbers that they went from birth to adulthood without being noticed?" [From the last chapter.]

NANCY: What we have to remember is that prior to the 1700s, there were very few violets—practically none. Blue was the top dog, and tan and yellow and green. The violets started getting more and more and more, just like the Indigos are doing now.

The vanguards are the violets. Do you see what I'm saying on that level? Almost every two centuries, a new color comes in, and that's what the civilization takes up. So the violets started really coming in strong during the 18th century. Prior to that, they were just smidgens for a while. It's just that time is speeding up, and these Indigos are doing it at a much faster rate than the other colors did.

The violets are the forerunners to the Indigos. Remember, they don't have a lesson; they're reviewing everything—some things half-remembered and some things half-forgotten. The Indigos are not reviewing; they're futurists. They're here to show us tomorrow. They don't give a hang about yesterday. But the violets had to weave everything together to complete the third dimension. So all the roles of the colors are very important to honor. Each one has its place and does not weaken the system in its own process. So that's what we have to know about that: The violets are the forerunners of the Indigos

Remember, from 2,000 years ago until the middle of the 20th century, we were strictly religious. *Metaphysics* was not a word that we used, even though Aristotle invented it. We were more religiously oriented, and even in the middle of the 20th century, what we now call metaphysics was called *spiritualism*—a Protestant process of the Christian faith. And weird people were under the eye of the vice squad, the same as prostitutes. So it's only in the last 100 years, let's say, that we've been able to be free thinkers outside the known Bible. So nobody ever talked about color; nobody ever talked about the development of the human mind on that level, or that we had a purpose in the Universe. We were just God's children.

So we have a process that's going on that is so much more dramatic and is moving so much faster in this time than ever before. We're still hooked on religion, and we're still not willing to give humans credit for their own evolution. We've taken quantum leaps in the last century on our mind development, yet we're feeling deficient because there's something new on the horizon. That always puzzles me—why do we have that? It's that we're just moving at a faster pace; therefore, our linear line of life is much more dramatic. It does exist now. It did not in the past. It was just such a smooth little ripple, and nobody really felt it. But now it's becoming almost like the computer in bytes, cuts, and moves. So we have to be aware of that. It's interesting.

JAN: Let's get to the kids. Since our last interview, more than two years have elapsed. Is there anything new regarding the Indigo Children that you're aware of or that has changed?

NANCY: I think they're getting more aware of who they are. One of the things I'm researching now that I just noticed this past year in Europe, is that I'm seeing a particular characteristic with most of the *humanists,* and that is that they have crooked teeth. That may sound kind of silly. The *humanists* often have crooked teeth where their mouth isn't big enough for the front tooth, and very few of them are getting it fixed. I've noticed that.

A lot of these Indigos are with families who are not putting braces on their children, and I don't know why, but I've been surprised by it because the children are 16, 17, 18, 20, or 22. Also, I see it in the younger ones. Now, I don't know whether the families will get them braces or not, but it doesn't seem to be an issue. The *artists* and the *conceptuals* do not have this.

JAN: Maybe the children really aren't concerned about how they look.

NANCY: I have no idea what it is. Well, I also think we're not as medically inclined now as we used to be. They [doctors] don't have the absolute rule anymore. That's the only change I've noticed, except that there are more and more of them [Indigos]. I think we'll see the biggest change in the next five or six years, but I don't think this is going to change the definition. I think it's going to define it more.

JAN: With your special gift, are you seeing any new colors?

NANCY: Not yet. But when I got the Indigo color, I was told that there would be another color, and I haven't seen it yet. I keep waiting.

JAN: Can you guess at what it might be?

NANCY: No, I can't even fathom it.

JAN: Since we published the Indigo book, there has been a tremendous increase in violence in terms of children killing children. How does this figure into the Indigo experience?

NANCY: Well, remember what I said. When we get to 100 percent, half will be building a utopia, and half a chaos. Half will be building a hell. And what I've noticed with all the children who have been killing other people is that they've been *conceptuals*, and the *conceptuals*, remember, are project oriented. People are just tools for their project. The thing I noticed about it most, with the exception of the two students who [allegedly] killed the [Dartmouth] college professors—and I haven't read the story enough to know their background and what they were doing because they were from the upper middle class—is that most of the time when they do it, the *conceptuals* kill themselves, too. There's something hidden in that other story, however, that I haven't gotten yet.

JAN: When was that story?

NANCY: That was last week. The father of one of the boys turned them in. They were on the run, but I think something took place that created that situation differently. However, they are *conceptuals,* both of them. As I say, I notice most of the time that they kill themselves, too. So that's why I think these two have a different story, and I'm going to be following it to find out what it is, because there's something not on the table yet.

JAN: Were they "on" anything?

NANCY: That's the question I want to ask. But I think a lot of them just have parents who have made them angry at the world

JAN: And they're exposing it to everyone?

NANCY: Look at the Indigos in school: If a parent abuses them, they'll go to school and tell someone and get help. A lot of them will call 911. A lot of them will tell the police, "My parents are beating me." They're more open about their process than we were. Somehow we had a built-in mechanism that said, "We can't tell anybody since it's *our* fault." These children don't buy that. It's happening at an even younger age now and is even more dramatic. The children now who are under ten are going to have things that other people never had.

I think we have to understand how fast we're moving, and how things are going on that many would have looked at in horror 15 years ago, even 10 years ago. So I think that we're going to see more and more of the fact that as the Indigos get more unified, there's going to be a sharp difference between the violet and the Indigo, and it will be very easily recognized—sort of the old versus the young. And we'll see it with respect to the new capabilities of their bodies as well as their minds.

JAN: Do you have any thoughts or evidence that the children of Indigos have anything added that the original Indigo children didn't have? In other words, do you feel that the spiritual evolvement of this human group can be seen?

NANCY: I think, yes, there is a definite difference. I don't know that I'd call it spiritual, because the younger the Indigos are, the more computerized they are, the more matter of fact they are, the more they distrust our world, the more they see us as failures, and the more they see that we have no process of honesty. I think that's one of the things we're all looking at.

JAN: Do you think it's that they're reading our minds, and we're saying one thing but many of us are thinking something else?

NANCY: Well, I don't know that they're reading our minds, but I think that their sensitivity level is much more acute than ours, and they sense things and they trust their senses. And we still get muddled up in it all. I call it: "We're still corruptible to the world." We oftentimes don't know what reality is. We only know our perception of it.

Line 15 people up, and we'll have 15 different perceptions. So truth has many faces. To the Indigos, truth has a different meaning. I think they're going to be far more androgynous than we were. Sex is not going to mean to them what it meant to us. They're not going to use it as a ploy to get married; they're going to use it for play, which is what I think it was originally intended for anyway, in addition to procreation. But they may not trust procreation as much as we did, which means that they may be interested in self-sufficiency first, which is the violet's lesson.

You know, the violet age demands that we be self-sufficient. The violets, most of them, are destination oriented. These children will love the journey, but the destination doesn't count. So a lot of parents are facing challenges with children graduating from high school who aren't yet ready to go to college—and don't want to. A lot of them are going to stay home until they can afford to live the way in which their parents have gotten them accustomed. Do you understand?

In our generations, we couldn't wait to leave home and start from scratch. We didn't want our parents' money. They wouldn't give it to us anyway. It was an achievement to get out and do it on our own. These children say, "I'll do it," and then they stay home. It's an interesting time. Therefore, their value system is going to be so totally different from ours that some people will see it as horrible, and some people will see it as wonderful. The truth is that they're changing, and they're going to show us what love is, and we're going to be really amazed that we lost it! They're going to show us how to enjoy living—not how to be run by the strong kids in the school—to be more in the moment and not so much concerned with whether they have a certificate or not, but doing what makes them happy. They're going to be much different.

JAN: That is what I call "living in harmony with the Inner Child," which was the piece of me that I found when my mother was making her transition called *death*. When I found my own Inner Child and started working with her, my life changed. I needed to *re-parent* her (the Inner Child). As she and I were releasing our physical world mother, I was able to help her and remind her that I was her real Mom/fairy God-mother.

NANCY: Now, think how many people do not do that.

JAN: So what I get from the Indigos is that these parents are trying to learn how to handle their kids, and what I'm getting is that they need to try to learn how to handle their Inner Child. If they get that, they have the other.

NANCY: I think you're absolutely right. Don't try to *be* them.

JAN: Get in touch with your inner one. The Indigo Children will see honesty and truth within you.

NANCY: Yes, and then the Indigos take care of the rest of it. Indigos like straight talk.

JAN: Absolutely.

NANCY: They don't like to be talked down to. I had a lady come in yesterday who's a screenwriter in Los Angeles, and she brought her 12-year-old son with her. So I'm sitting and chatting with him, and she says, "You know, he will tell *you* the truth. He won't tell anybody else." He'll just talk to me, but he won't talk to her. So she brings him down so she can find out what he's doing. Isn't that funny?

JAN: I love it. Thank you again, Nancy.

c h a p t e r   f i v e

The Inner Child

*"A society in which adults are estranged from the world
of children, and often from their own childhood, tends to hear
children's speech only as a foreign language, or as a lie. . . .
Children have been treated . . . as congenital fibbers,
fakers and fantasizes."*

— **Beatrix Campbell**, British journalist[1]

We're now going to broach a subject that you may be
familiar with, but which many of you may not fully
understand. What does one's Inner Child work have to do
with the subject of raising and interacting with Indigo
Children? In this discussion, we're going to try to zero in on
that exact question.

What can you do to fully understand this chapter? What
else—become warm and fuzzy—think back to the time when
you were a six- or seven-year-old. What? You can't remember?
That's the main issue, isn't it?

After a recent workshop we presented on the East Coast,
a man came up to Jan and asked if he could join her at the
lunch break. He started the conversation with tears in his
eyes. He explained that after attending one of our other
workshops a year earlier, he had experienced the personal
awakening of a lifetime.

David was in his middle 50s, and unlike most men his age, he was becoming very emotional as he told his story. "Jan," he said, "you know my wife and I have attended many of your workshops. We always enjoy them. However, in the last one, you spoke of your experience of discovering your Inner Child. As you encouraged the attendees to get comfortable and began to start your guided meditation, I found myself expecting a pleasant, relaxing experience. This time, though, you directed us to explore that piece of us called 'the Inner Child.' I tried to stay out of judgment, but truthfully, I didn't quite accept the concept. In honor to you both, however, I kept my eyes closed and stayed with the program. To my astonishment, a sad, bedraggled, angry little boy appeared to me in my mind. He told me I had buried him in my backyard, from the time I had come back from Vietnam. He was very angry at me. I burst into tears—something I would not normally do."

David wanted to tell Jan his recollection and thank her in person, since it the experience had made such a profound impression on him. She asked him if his experience had made any difference after that as applied to normal life. He told her that he had made an agreement with his newly found "child" to purchase a Harley Davidson motorcycle so "they" could take long, fun, "wind" rides in the country.

Jan then asked him, "Has anyone accused you of going through a midlife crisis?" He said that some do think so, but when he answers them, his new *kid* (little David) answers them playfully—not defensively.

Little David often tells them, "We're going through mid-youth rebirthing!" He went on to tell Jan that he felt far more spontaneous as a new person. He felt playful, and humor was a much more important part of his life than it had ever been before. David said, "I laugh a lot now."

*"A childlike man is not a man whose development
has been arrested; on the contrary, he is a man
who has given himself a chance of continuing
to develop long after most adults have muffled themselves
in the cocoon of middle-aged habit and convention."*

— *Aldous Huxley*[1]

Who is the Inner Child? Who or what is that piece of a human that can get buried in the backyard for most of one's lifetime? Sometimes this burial is for life, never to be found. Why are we even talking about this? After all, this book is about *real* kids, isn't it?

As we were gathering information about the first Indigo book, an interesting thought occurred to us—one we alluded to in that book. We came to the conclusion that Indigos are here for many reasons. One, which may sound a bit subtle, is that they may be here to help us find our own inner children. Why? Because the Indigos will respond more positively to the "real selves" of the parents.

In Chapter 2, Moneque LeBlanc wrote about Indigos sensing true feelings. The following story is very similar to Moneque's, but this one is from Bea Wragee, whom we met earlier.

"Why Are You So Angry, Mommy?"
Bea Wragee

One afternoon I went into my five-year-old son's room with some laundry. Trey looked at me curiously and said, "Why are you so angry, Mommy?" Surprised,

> I answered, "I'm not mad, honey." He looked at me with riveting eyes and replied, "Then why do you have that mad look on your face?"
>
> He was responding to the truth that showed so clearly in my face. The truth was the truth! I was angry, and his sensitivity to my body language and expressions was accurate. Now, could I be enough of an adult to admit it? Would I discount his reality or honor his awareness?
>
> Mustering some courage, I told him, "You're right, honey, I am angry about something that happened today, and I didn't tell you the truth. I apologize."
>
> My son's gift to me that day was awareness of being my *whole self,* and to be honest about things. How can you teach a child to tell the truth if you're unable to do it yourself?

Do you see how intuitive Bea's son was? What was happening here? The Indigos are finely tuned to "see" the energy of their mirror within the adult. They want to look at any human, adult or otherwise, and see the child portion. We are calling this the "real self," or "whole self," and feel that it's the common denominator for communication with the Indigos.

Let's look at an academic definition of the Inner Child according to Charles L. Whitfield, M.D., author of *Healing the Child Within:*[6]

> The concept of the Child Within has been a part of world culture for at least two thousand years. Carl Jung called it the "Divine Child," and Emmet Fox called it the "Wonder Child." Psychotherapist Alice Miller and Donald Winnicott referred to it as the "True Self." Rokelle Learner and others in the field of chemical dependency call it the "Inner Child." The Child Within refers to that part of each of us which is ultimately alive, energetic, creative and fulfilled; it is our Real Self—who we really are.

As we're growing up, many of us sometimes need to bury ourselves, or part of ourselves, "in the backyard" in order to survive. The "real self" retreats from us, often being as close as the backyard, but not in the house with us. Have you ever felt as if something was missing in your life? We mean something that's a core issue, not a partner or money. Did you ever feel as if there was part of *you* that was missing? That's the indication that perhaps your Inner Child went into hiding.

Here is where the Indigo Children come into this in a profound way. Remember in the first book where we told you that Indigos are primarily left-right-brain balanced? With their innate awareness, they often recognize a "wounding" in their parents. They see that the Inner Child of the parent is missing, or not fully aware. They long for balance (as we have indicated before), and when it isn't there, a blockage in communication occurs. When the Inner Child is buried in us, we are separated not only from ourselves and others, but also from our Indigo Children!

How "wounded" can you be? Picture this: What if you just lost your firstborn child. Think about it. How devastating! Some of you know this kind of sorrow and grief and fully understand what it means. It's a life-changing energy, and it's part of you forever. Although the burying of the Inner Child may not compare to the loss of a real child, some of the attributes are the same. Do you retreat from others? Do you hide your feelings? Do you have difficulty nurturing new friendships? Do you feel sick a lot? Are you tired all the time? Are you often angry for no reason? Do you tend to keep running instead of walking or stopping to breathe, preventing you from examining what's around you? Do you get fearful easily? Are you lonely all the time? Is your life humorless? Is everything "a drag"?

Answer this question *true* or *false:* Adults work; kids play.

If you said "true," then perhaps you should continue reading. These are classic symptoms of the loss of love, and also the burial of the child within.

The classic example of looking for the pony in the pile of manure is still the best story we can cite in this regard: A child enters the room with the expectation of seeing the pony. He's been told that the pony is there. The manure is secondary, and is something that doesn't get in the way. The child excitedly digs for the pony, giggling the whole time—and finds it! The adult also knows the pony is there, but often sees the manure first and either stops the whole experience, or complains about the stench the whole time. The experience is about the manure, not the pony. Where are you in this example?

Okay, we're adults. We acknowledge that the pressures and responsibilities we have are far greater than what a child experiences on a daily basis. However, what we're promoting here is a self-examination of your own balance. Without the inner kid, there may not be any! Did anyone every call you a grump or a spoiler? Did a child ever say that to you? (Probably a very wise kid!)

Some of you are saying, "Not me. I had a happy childhood." The truth is that many of us had imperfect childhoods, some even dysfunctional in certain ways. Growing up might have been painful for you. That's when you decided to "dig the hole" and "jump in" so that pieces of you could survive within the dysfunctional situations. When this occurred, you became disconnected from "real self" and often drew away from those around you.

As we grow up, we often take as our truth what we've heard from those around us in authority positions—parents, teachers, counselors; and even books, movies, and TV. Hopefully we started to better discern our truth as we grew older.

By now, however, the old programming is still present, lurking in our personalities, no longer really serving us well. For instance, as a child, you might have been told not to play with fire. Now you wish to design sculptures using a blowtorch. You need to reevaluate the old "tapes" in order to release the fear or emotions that would keep you from your new desire to create a sculpture using fire.

What is the primary attribute of a healthy Inner Child? Not to oversimplify all of this (since much has been written about it), but it's balance. A person with a healthy Inner Child is spontaneous, creative, playful, blissful, and is able to laugh openly at their own situation. In our opinion, this is also someone who's in touch with whatever they call God, a spiritual acknowledgment of Spirit. There's much more, but you get the picture.

When you travel on an airplane, the flight attendant instructs you on using the oxygen mask. They're supposed to fall down from above if the cabin loses pressure. If you have a child with you, the flight attendant tells you, "Take care of yourself first, then your child." We have the same message. Given the pressures of life, you absolutely must take care of yourself first in order to care for that precious cargo that Spirit has given you to steward.

Okay, so what's the task at hand? Let's say that the cabin of this metaphoric airplane is in the dark when the pressure is lost. Therefore, there are two steps we have to take before we can help our child: (1) Find your mask, and (2) put it on!

The Backyard—Finding the Buried Kid

Finding the buried kid is a metaphor for admitting that the child is *not* in your life. Almost simultaneously, your realization that the kid is hidden will precipitate the search and recovery. Here is something to consider: Most of our verbalization to children is often to emphasize their growing up. The adult gets the attention. For instance, when a parent talks to their crying son, you often hear, "Don't cry; be a big boy." Have you ever heard a single mother say to her male child, "You're Mommy's little man"? The honoring seems to relate to being an adult. Although we say these things to children because we think they will respond to something obvious—the desire to be grown up—it often negates the importance of being a child. It's time to acknowledge the fertile richness of the "child-self" in both the children and in us.

There's quite a bit of irony here. If you could really examine the innermost thoughts of children, there are some experts who will tell you that kids are very wise about all this—that although they yearn for the privileges associated with being older, they also perceive the unhappiness often inherent in adulthood, sometimes reflected in their own family experience. They actually may not wish to be anything but a child! What we're examining is the ability of any adult to reclaim some of the childlike attributes that were so grand, many of which are there, but buried.

"The child thinks of growing old as an almost obscene calamity, which for some mysterious reason will never happen to itself. All who have passed the age of thirty are joyless, grotesque, endlessly fussing about things of no importance and staying alive without, so far as the child can see, having anything to live for. Only child life is real life."

— **George Orwell**[1]

We'd like to let you know about a great book that discusses finding the buried child in a step-by-step fashion, and it's one of the best Inner Child books currently published. The title is *Recovery of Your Inner Child*,[7] by Lucia Capacchione, Ph.D. Here is what Dr. Capacchione says about the Inner Child, which will give you an idea of how important it is:

> *"To be fully human, the child within must be embraced and expressed."*

Let's go on a treasure hunt! Now the words *treasure hunt* will probably tantalize your Inner One. What we're doing here is helping you find the real treasure—you! We're going to look at just a couple of methods that others are successfully teaching. If you're serious about this, then don't let the ceremony or newness of these methods put you off. They work!

Following is a technique from Sharyl Jackson, an eight-year veteran of public school teaching. Sharyl was raised on a farm in North Dakota, received her undergraduate degree in languages from the University of North Dakota and her master's degree in Spanish literature from the University of Washington. She spent eight years as a public school teacher before working with the juvenile justice program in Seattle. Sharyl has raised a houseful of now grown Indigo Children, and she's been on her personal journey of remembering for many years. Her remarks were first published on the Internet [**www.PlanetLighworker.com**], and are used with permission.

Your Inner Child and Your Indigo Child
Sharyl Jackson

I suggest you begin your communication with your Inner Child by creating a quiet, safe, relaxed time and space. I also suggest in the beginning that your words be spoken aloud and include a statement about your intentions.

We interrupt Sharyl's discourse to give you a sample of what that intent might sound like. "I call upon God, Spirit, Divine Love, to fill my being. I ask in purity to call forth my Inner Child." Use whatever words are meaningful to you. This is not a religious statement, but one that calls upon your core spiritual feeling to show that your intent is pure in finding this potentially hidden treasure.

I also think it's important to clean the slate, so to speak, so tell your Inner Child that you're beginning a new form of communication with it ["it"is being used instead of him/her]. Say that you're sorry for all the times you didn't pay attention, didn't protect it, abandoned it, whatever comes to you that you feel this part of you wants and needs to hear. You may also wish to verbalize that you forgive it for all of the pain and suffering in the body as well as the blocks it has put in your life. Please do not rush this part of the process, since communication, clarity, and trust are crucial to success.

When you feel you've set the stage and are ready for a dialogue, begin by asking verbally or silently what your Inner Child's name is. Accept the first thing you hear, sense, or know, and don't be surprised by anything. Continue this conversation with simple questions such as favorite foods, colors, whatever. In other words, spend time learning to communicate, and build an atmosphere of trust. As time goes by, you'll be able to engage in more in-depth and meaningful conversations. It's your job to create safety for this Child, as well as to assure it that it's loved and nourished. The Child will assist you greatly in creating joy, harmony, health and well-being, and yes, even miracles, if you will include them in your life.

At the very least, spend some time thinking about how you wished you had been treated as a child. These are important clues to loving and effective parenting, whether in relation to your Inner Child or any child in your care. I can assure you that any effort you devote to this Inner Child work will reap great benefits for all. If you're being challenged by your Indigo, put these new skills to use for clearer communication. If you're a wonderful parent of your Indigo, think what you're doing for them that you might not be doing for your own inner kid. Again, I cannot stress enough how important this work is in our own personal growth, as well as harmony in the home and the world.

Now, back to the actual experience of finding the Inner Kid. At another recent workshop of ours, Jillian, a 57-year-old woman, spoke to Jan. Jillian has been a diabetic for the last 30 years, regularly injecting herself with insulin. She craved sweets, of course, and often indulged herself regardless of her intent not to. Although Jillian realized how bad this was for her, she was often unsuccessful in her attempts to avoid sugary treats.

Jan suggested that she "get quiet"; take some deep, slow, full breaths; and ask for support from Spirit, whatever that meant to her. Jan could see that Jillian was a meditator, so what followed would make sense to her. She was instructed to ask her "little child within" what it was trying to tell her with respect to these sugar cravings—which were obviously detrimental to her health. If there was anything the child liked as much as the sugar, what was it? Could she get in touch with herself in this regard to actually receive the answer?

Jillian tried. She became quiet, and in a few moments, she responded, telling a story. Evidently she'd had a brother who had died of a heart condition before she was born. As a young child, she had a depressed mother—one who wouldn't let Jillian do much of anything physical, fearing a repeat of the tragedy with her son. Jillian, however, lived for her ballet lessons, which were discontinued as a result of her mother's fear. It seems that Jillian's Inner Child was still mourning this fact. With this came the realization that her own diabetic symptoms started with the birth of her own second child! This is what her Inner Child told her: *"I love to dance! I really miss being able to dance. Dancing was so sweet and fun. Could we please dance?"*

As a result, Jillian found more room in her life to dance, and her sugar cravings actually diminished, as though her body somehow understood that the needs of the Inner Child had been heard and honored. In review, this started with intent, and resulted in a wonderful solution.

The Power of Your Other Hand [8]

The Power of Your Other Hand is the title of still another book by Dr. Capacchione. It's also a method that's reprised in her book *Recovery of Your Inner Child,*[7] mentioned earlier.

Some of you are not meditators, so you might be wondering if there's an exercise that can help you get answers like Jillian did. The answer is yes! It's a fun one developed by Dr. Capacchione, and it has worked successfully for many. Here's what she had to say:

> Our non-dominant hand has atrophied from lack of use, and has stayed frozen at a very early stage of development. The paradox is that it is this retarded "other hand" that can lead us back to our Inner Child. . . . You're opening up your right hemisphere. [Of the brain] . . . Each hemisphere of the human brain controls the opposite side of the body. It also appears that there are specialized functions for each half of the brain. The left-brain contains language centers that control verbal and analytical processing. It has been described as the linear and logical side of the brain. By contrast, the right-brain appears to be primarily non-verbal and governs visual/spatial perception, as well as emotional expression and intuition. My observations show that writing with the non-dominant hand directly accesses right-brain functions. . . . When we write dialogs [sic] between the Child (non-dominant hand) and the adult or Inner Parent (dominant hand), we seem to be conversing between the two hemispheres of the brain.

Dr. Capacchione believes that through her extensive work in Inner Child discovery, that writing with the frozen, or nondominant hand, directly accesses right-brain functions. One of the writings techniques she uses is what she calls "dialoguing with both hands."

She asks us to write a conversation using both hands. You, as the adult, will write with your dominant hand (the hand you normally write with). Your Inner Child will write or print with your other, nondominant hand. You start by verbally giving intent to your Inner Kid to "know him or her." Ask the name of the child, and anything else the Child wants to tell you. For instance, how it feels, how old it is, and anything it wants to share with you. Second, ask the Child to draw a picture of what it wants most at this time in your life. Finally, close the communication by asking, "Is there anything else it wants you to know?" Close by thanking the Child and telling it that there will be more conversations to come. During this conversation, remember: The child is always right. It's expressing feelings, which are not positive or negative—they're just feelings.

We told you that this would be wild. But the results, according to Dr. Capacchione, are profound. We add that this is an exercise that should be repeated each day, even if it's only for ten minutes. Set aside a time that's quiet, like right before bedtime. We also suggest putting up the Child's photo during the conversation. This helps you focus on whatever age it told you it was. Dr. Capacchione also suggests keeping the drawing the Child made during the first interview at all subsequent sessions.

How to Converse with Your Inner Child (recap)

1. Go to a safe place, one where you can be quiet and peaceful. Breathe deeply and bring yourself to a beautiful place in your mind that feels serene.

2. Verbally give intent, out loud, to *know* and find this Inner Child.

3. Use your dominant hand as the adult to ask the questions.

4. Use your nondominant hand as the Child to answer.

5. Use your third hand to conduct the band! Oops—that was our Kid talking (hee-hee).

6. Ask the Child its name and to draw a picture of itself. Be patient and take your time. Don't laugh. Be loving and patient as you would with any child.

7. Ask the other questions (as indicated above).

8. Close by asking the final question ("What is it you want me to know?"), and by thanking the Child for coming out and talking.

9. Tell the Child that there will be more conversations soon.

To be privy to some wonderful conversations between adult and Child, be certain to get Dr. Capacchione's book. The conversations are revealing, sweet, sometimes heavy, but very rewarding.

Re-parenting

Now that you've found the Child and are talking to it, it's time to reestablish the relationship you always wanted. This is called re-parenting, and stands for "putting on the mask" in the metaphor we gave you earlier regarding the oxygen mask in the airplane.

What does it mean? Quite simply, it's the method for setting the standard of parenting for this Inner Child, which you, as a child, always desired. What would the "perfect parent" do? The perfect parent listens, takes time to play, tells two stories instead of one, and honors the kid with time to talk.

Naturally there's much more, but it requires getting rid of the "old tapes," the ones that make the parent the "critical parent" or the "authority." The beauty of this is that at this time in your life, you're all grown up. This means that all those things that were an issue when the child was learning about life are now done. This actually simplifies the process.

What can you do to begin re-parenting? Here are a few ways:

1. Allow your Inner Kid as much time for communication as it wants.

2. Get messy! We mean it. Go play in the dirt. Plant something. Draw something fun and stupid. Don't worry about staying inside the lines when you color.

3. Sing, dance, play a musical instrument, do art projects.

4. Go dancing! If you don't dance, that's even better. Go make dumb moves and be silly. People won't think you're strange; they will see your joy and playfulness. They'll probably envy you.

5. Don't be surprised if you meet other Kids along the way. When you do, play with them!

6. Allow the Inner Kid to dress you once in a while. (Yep, it's time to wear the funny shirt you bought at Disneyland.)

The Disney movie *The Kid* with Bruce Willis exemplifies everything we're talking about. The adult Bruce Willis unexpectedly meets his Inner Child on his doorstep. Then he begins the process we've described—that is, recognizing and listening to the Child. Along the way, he discovers that it's not all that easy, but when he finally lets the Kid in, he reframes and rewrites the past, which, of course, affects the present. He starts the movie as the *critical* parent, and slowly moves his way toward becoming the *nurturing* parent. Although the movie was a fantasy of sorts, the metaphor related to the concept is profoundly true.

chapter   six

About Parenting

(Today's children need more—have you noticed?)

W hat follows are two discussions from qualified individuals who are "in the trenches." They're working
with children and parents daily, and they're writing these
thoughts for us during a time when school shootings seem
to be an almost weekly occurrence.

We honor parents all over the world who are in the
process of discovery—searching for something entirely
different for their children than they got from their own
parents. This is not due to the fact that they were raised
poorly! One of the most frustrating feelings many mothers
and fathers experience is that they feel they're doing a good
job, just like their parents did, and something's not working.

Do these children need something more than what we
received? The answer is yes, but it's not that difficult to
figure out what it is. It's based on love, logic, and friendship.
It has to do with listening and being aware. It's takes self-
discipline, wisdom, and some other attributes that are
difficult to come by in a very busy, harried lifestyle—which
has come to be the norm in a society such as ours.

Dear parents, you're not alone in your frustration, and these
books we're writing are not meant to "finger point" at you. We
just want to help you become best friends with your precious

children, even if you think there has been "too much water under the bridge," and that as teens, they're "lost." Reports from parents all over the world say that this is not the case. It's never too late to show children love. However, they must really see the change in *you* before it will mean anything to them.

Here's a piece about parenting from a woman named Barbra Gilman. She has 20 years' experience as a therapist and is a Certified Parent Educator with the International Network for Children and Families. She is an interfaith minister and CEO of Success Strategies for Life. Barbra served as the director of the Center for Spiritual Awareness in New York and has hosted her own radio show, "Conscious Choices." She is a motivational speaker who has taught hundreds of workshops on personal and spiritual development and success through awareness. Her new book is called *The Unofficial Guide to Living Successfully on Planet Earth.* She can be reached at (888) 826-8930.

Training Parents
Peace Begins at Home: Wisdom and Support for Parents of Indigos
Barbra Gilman

First, a poem from a young man:

To My Parents:
You love me, So you think this gives you rights
To mold my life like yours.
But this can never be. I must be free, I must be me!
I know I'll make mistakes,

And whimper in my sleep.
For all things you as parents
Wish you could prevent
And yet I'm not your pet.
You cannot teach me tricks to come at your command,
Or always lead me by the paw or hand.
To win or fail, I alone must blaze my sometimes lonely,
Sometimes hurting trail.
— *Sef Tritt*, age 14

What if every child who came into the world was born with a personalized manual attached to their little toe? What if all new parents could take a series of vaccinations that inoculated them against repeating their parents' mistakes? What if all the people who cared for children—whether parents, grandparents, teachers or friends—were issued a special device that enabled them to be clairvoyant, ensuring that they would never again mistreat or misinterpret the intentions of a child for any reason? What if every child who was born grew up healthy, happy, peaceful, and free? What kind of world would this be?

Well, there are no personalized toe tag manuals, clairvoyance devices, or vaccinations to help us parent. There are no guarantees that any of us are even emotionally ready to become parents when we do. For the most part, we simply step into parenthood, hoping for the best. And to our credit, let me say that in my opinion, most of us strive to do our very best at all times, and often against tremendous odds. It's just that too often, our best is simply not enough to prevent the unhealthy patterns we have inherited from being passed on to our children.

So what can we do about it?

The Post-Modern Family

As parents, it may very well be our duty to pay attention, not just to our children—but also, and perhaps primarily—to ourselves, our own needs, and our own hurts. In fact, it's most likely that every person who reads this article has at least one painful memory of a time when their parents completely misunderstood them or did exactly the opposite of what they needed to grow into a balanced person with solidly healthy self-esteem. Some of us have many more than one memory. And for others, the painful memories far outweigh the sweet ones.

Yet, when most of us become parents, we assume that we will just know what to do, or that doing what our parents have done will be enough for our children. But we do not "just know" how to parent, and repeating what our parents have done while raising us is as likely to pass on damage to our children as it is to nurture their development into healthy, whole, and balanced persons.

Even those of us who were raised in loving and supportive environments may be at a loss as we face the demands of living in our society. Many families can no longer survive on a single income. With both parents working, family dinners and many of the other simple, stabilizing, and connective rituals of family life are lost. To compensate for the absence of togetherness, parents often opt for over-enrolling their children in extracurricular activities. The result is what I call "the Post-Modern Family": a group of people living under the same roof but going off in so many different directions that they barely have the opportunity to develop real intimacy. Post-Modern Families become disconnected instead of interconnected. Sometimes, family members don't seem to know each other at all.

As we enter the new millennium, the forces that govern human evolution have thrown a new element into the mix, a new gift for the future of humanity, and a new challenge for us all to embrace: the Indigo Children.

These new souls are coming on board in order to facilitate our transition to the next stage in the evolution of human consciousness. They are highly sensitive multi-dimensional beings, often with many talents and refined intuitive powers. More than ever in the span of recorded history, our children are different from us. They are, as one woman said, gazing at an Indigo infant, "born knowing."

Honesty Is Crucial

What is it that the Indigo Children know that most of us do not? Indigo Children instinctively know who they are and what they need. They know how human beings are supposed to treat each other. They expect people to be honoring and respectful. They do not under any circumstances respond well to lies, manipulation, or violence. Indigo children expect explanations, and often will not settle for "Because I said so." Also, they do best when addressed in all ways as if they were adults.

"But I don't lie to my kids! I don't manipulate! I'm not violent!" I can hear the chorus of voices right now. Most of us have never intentionally deceived our children, or used their self-esteem as a lever to control their behavior; and most of us have never raised a hand to a child in anger. However, sociologists, psychologists, and cultural critics from many fields have observed that our culture itself is steeped in violence, deception, and manipulation. How aware are we of the small but powerful ways in which our lives may personally be affected by the cultural messages that have indoctrinated certain habits in our minds from early childhood on?

We may not directly deceive our children until we feel that keeping some information from them is for their own good. At this point, we begin to digress from truthfulness, and most of us don't even think twice about it.

Let's look at the myth of Santa Claus. Santa Claus is so widely accepted that even many children who are not raised Christian still recognize and celebrate him. As a symbol, Santa has a popular appeal that transcends religious affiliation. But what if I were to tell you that behind this gentle old man in a fluffy red hat is a violent, manipulative lie designed to help adults control children's behavior and maintain the status quo? Extreme, you say? Well, let's take a look.

Santa brings all the bounty of unconditional love to children each Christmas, or does he? Santa's symbolic sack is overflowing, but the myth that most of us know from our childhoods is that if we aren't good, Santa won't bring us anything. So, if you're not good, Santa will take all of your gifts away. This is not unconditional love at all. What Santa becomes in this context is an enculturated form of punishment, a lie both psychically violent and manipulative to children.

Now again, this may seem extreme to some of us, and we may even tell ourselves that children don't take any of this seriously enough for it to harm them in any way. That is a dangerous assumption. One of the lessons I teach in my work with parents is to look at the world through the eyes of our children. To young children, this story is not a myth—it is very, very real. And while the use of Santa to control behavior gives at best a message to be externally motivated; at worst, it teaches obedience through fear of lack and the withdrawal of love and acceptance.

I became strikingly aware of this dynamic when a mother told me this story about her daughter, a 12-year-old Indigo Child. Mother and daughter were driving to a shop when the song "Santa Claus Is Comin' to Town" came on the radio. Mom was just bopping her head, replaying happy childhood memories of snowstorms and hot chocolate when her daughter, Kim, exclaimed "That's child abuse, Mom! What a terrible song!"

"I'll tell you, I was flabbergasted," Kim's mom told me. "I never thought of Santa Claus in the same way again."

Now Santa Claus is, at heart, a symbol of giving and of grace. Celebrate Santa surely, just don't use him as a threat or a reward. Let him be a symbol of abundance and the miracles that truly spring from unconditional love.

We have to wake up to the messages that we were raised with, messages that many of us blindly accepted even though they may have been harmful to us in subtle ways—messages that may have helped our parents to control our behavior but which will be increasingly useless to influence the Indigo generations. I'm not trying to convince you to ban Santa Claus from your family in order to be good parents. Of course not! But I do hope to convince you that as parents, we need to become aware: Old methods of discipline and control are no longer effective. If we can accept that these new children are here to teach us, and if we can learn to see through their eyes, all of our lives will change for the better.

Different Perspectives

Do children really see things so differently? Yes, they do. And not just as teenagers.

Another mother I worked with shared a story about

how her six-year-old son came up to her one day and asked, "Mommy why don't you love me anymore?"

Surprised and perplexed, the mother said, "Of course I love you, Danny! Why would you think I don't love you?"

Danny answered, "Because you only read me one story at bedtime now, and you used to read me two."

It never occurred to this busy mother that such a simple change in routine could leave her son feeling so hurt and unloved. She certainly had no intention of hurting her little one. She was just an ordinary overworked parent, trying to fit everything in to her day. And like so many of us, she just didn't think about how her little boy was wired to perceive reality, but she *did* take the time to listen to what he had to say and to honor his feelings. Now, Danny knows that he is still loved even though patterns sometimes change. But before Danny's mom took my class, she didn't know how important it was to listen to his feelings, and her habit was simply to brush him off, telling him, "Oh that's not important, sweetie, how silly to think that!" When she learned how to get down to his level and see the world with him, eye-to-eye, the mysteries of his universe were unveiled to her, and she could understand how deeply he felt. She could help him adjust without trauma.

We already know that when traumatized, whether by mistreatment or simple misunderstanding, Indigo Children tend to end up on Ritalin and other similar drugs designed for behavior modification. This kind of Band-Aid response to the needs and demands of our young people may make the school day and the afternoon at home more manageable, but how does it help our kids? It doesn't. What it does is help adults maintain the status quo.

But what is the status quo that adults are seeking to maintain? Is our world so perfectly balanced, so filled with peace and love, that we can afford not to question our choices? Can we honestly choose to ignore the possibility that if our children are having difficulties, we might be the ones who need to change? I don't think so. In fact, I believe that the future of our world depends on parents, teachers, and other adults who care about the welfare of children, developing the insight and behavior necessary to empower young people to develop their abilities to the utmost. And we need to be able to do this in full awareness that in many instances we have no idea what many of these abilities are because the Indigo Children are often gifted in such novel ways.

What can we do? Educate ourselves. Read about the Indigo Children. Explore our own childhood experiences, both positive and negative. Grow as people.

The course I teach, Redirecting Children's Behavior (RCB), is a five-week training program designed to help parents make the changes they need in their own lives so that they can change their relationships with their children for the better. How can you teach your child positive self-talk if you go around all day running a self-critical diatribe in your own head? You can't! Especially not around the highly sensitive Indigo Children—they'll smell hypocrisy in a heartbeat, and the lesson will be over before lunch. So RCB begins by teaching parents how to develop positive self-talk and then helping them learn how to model this skill for their children. It's like learning a new language.

How can you be an example of self-respect and consideration for others when your life is so stressful that you never have time to take care of yourself? You can't! So RCB begins by teaching parents how to make the time to love and nurture themselves. An overstressed person is like a well that has been tapped dry. When we learn to refill ourselves on a regular basis, we can better nurture and refresh those around us. And when we truly love ourselves, we're simply more sincerely loving to everyone else in our lives.

If we want to learn to support children's dreams, give them focused attention, take the time to honor their true intentions, respect their boundaries, openly express affection, allow them to experience natural consequences rather than punishments or rewards, use mistakes as an opportunity to encourage them—we need to learn how to replenish the well of our spirit. But how? The RCB course teaches us how to guide our children by first joining with them, learning to see the world from their point of view. Our Indigo Children will happily lead the way, so play, celebrate, create, and explore! Children innately sense that the key to healing and restoring the spirit is in the free and uninhibited expression of the simple joy of being alive. We only have to allow our children to be our guides.

Well, it's not always an easy task: From childhood on, so many of us are taught to "grow up," and as soon as we graduate or land that special job or pop out that baby, we start telling ourselves, "So now I'm an adult."

We begin to model "adult" behaviors and take on "adult" responsibilities. We grow up too much, and we lose touch with the curious, creative, and adventurous part of ourselves. Another mother told me a story about spending an afternoon with her seven-year-old daughter and two of her daughter's friends. It was a warm, rainy day, and all the kids were inside tearing up the house. This mother was a pretty dedicated mom and didn't resort to television, but things were really getting out of hand. She found herself becoming more and more stern and more and more stressed, saying no in every other sentence, her voice rising.

Suddenly, in a kind of epiphany, she realized how miserable she was and threw herself onto the couch in a mock temper tantrum, beating her fists and yelling, "I don't want to be a grown-up anymore. I hate being a grown-up and having to say no all the time. I just want to be a kid and have fun!"

The room became very quiet. All three little girls just stared at her. Then everyone started to laugh. "Come on," she said, "let's go run around the block in the rain!" And they did. Three times.

They had hot showers and hot chocolate afterwards. For the rest of the day, the kids all read and played quietly together. And from time to time, over the next two years, Mom would hear her daughter tell the story of when she and her mother and her two friends went running around the block together in the rain—three times! That's how much this little adventure meant to her child.

But it meant even more to Mom. What this mother found was a really wonderful part of herself, one that could play and be spontaneous. She had reconnected with her Inner Child.

I hesitated to use the term *Inner Child* in this essay because the concept has been given so much publicity over the past 15 years or so that many of us have stopped listening. "Oh, that," we say, and simply tune out. What we don't realize is that we're not just tuning out the idea or catch phrase; we're tuning out the Inner Child yet again!

Poor thing! Just imagine how you would feel: You're four years old and you're at the center of a huge publicity blitz; everyone who is anyone wants to read about you, play with you, and learn from you. You have practically no privacy at all. Then, gradually, all your new "friends" say, "Well, that's that then—'life' is calling."

Next thing you know, everyone goes back to their grown-up lives, forgetting about you completely. You were just getting used to all the attention, and now you're alone again. How would you feel? Confused? Hurt? Lost? Unloved?

The point I'm rather fancifully making is that in order to truly integrate such a fragile part of ourselves back into the core of awareness, we can't just take a weekend holiday and presume the quality of our lives will change for the long term—we have to work at it, or rather, play at it, daily.

I once had a woman in my seminar, let's call her Ms. Perfection. She was a great lady, very powerful and successful at work, but quite robotic in her body language. She seemed a nice enough woman, but not warm, as if she had a wall over her heart. So I gave her an exercise: For a week, she needed to visualize herself as a clown. She did pretty well, so the following week, I actually had her go to a party store, buy a big red nose, tie a scarf around her neck, wear a funny hat, and start interacting with her children in that way. The next time I saw her, she said that her 13-year-old son told her that he had never felt this close to her before. "Whatever you're doing in your life to make these changes, Mom," he said, "thank you."

A month or so later, she called to tell me that she had received a promotion that she never even thought was possible. What had happened? The company told her, we don't know what you did, but something's different!

This is how it works: One simple step of getting in touch with the Inner Child and putting that connection into daily practice can change every aspect of a person's life. In all the years of working with people, I've noticed that the folks who absolutely get in there and do work on the Inner Child create the most miraculous changes.

Ms. Perfection was willing to make a change and to *practice* that change, which is the real key.

If we have the courage to be honest with ourselves and our kids, we can create a passageway to a new life for parents and children alike. The Indigo Children know what they need, and if we stay open and learn to listen without defensiveness, they will tell us. Honesty, trust, openness, and sincerity can be grounded in simple, behavioral steps if parents are willing to begin with themselves. Taking a child's point of view seriously may be new to many of us, but it maybe precisely an Indigo point of view that our world needs most. And just like Ms. Perfection's son, Indigos never miss it when their parents take sincere steps toward building a more peaceful world, because they instinctively know the greatest secret: Peace begins at home.

Sometimes
Sometimes life turns around and slaps you upside
    the head . . .
    and it hurts.
Sometimes love rips your heart from your chest and
    throws you in the deep end . . .
    and you learn to move on.
Sometimes you can't find yourself in your mind . . .
    and you smile.
Sometimes dreams come true but no one is there to
    pinch you . . .
    and you keep dreaming.
— *Kat,* age 13

Here's a fascinating story by Shirley Michael about an Indigo named Amber. Dr. Michael's education includes an M.A. in counseling and a Ph.D. in transpersonal psychology; and a background in Eastern and Western nutrition, body somatics, vibrational medicine, aromatherapy, color and sound therapies, bio-physics, energetics, and dance/movement therapy. She maintains a private counseling practice and leads workshops and seminars on a variety of subjects. Her articles on health and healing are regularly published. She is the mother of an Indigo, her most educational experience to date!

For further information, Dr. Michael can be reached via e-mail at: **smichael@znet.com.**

Drugs, Death, and Life Ever After
Shirley Michael, M.A., Ph.D.

The call from a frantic mother came in the morning. Her 13-year-old daughter had threatened the family with kitchen knives, and they were terrified. What should they do?

When 13-year-old Amber arrived at my office, she looked like many teenage girls: long hair, no makeup, nondescript clothing. Her demeanor was self-contained, and there was a spark of curiosity in her brown eyes. Her mother left, as I had requested. I wanted to be alone with Amber, and I said I would call her parents later that evening.

I thanked Amber for coming and told her I was not going to make her "wrong," and I understood it took courage for her to come and visit me, a stranger. Furthermore, I was not on her parents' side, and was only interested in helping the situation if she wanted me to. It was her choice. She looked me straight in the eyes, and said, "Okay."

When I asked her why she had agreed to come and see me, she said she scared herself with some of her actions, and she didn't want to hurt anyone, but she felt like "a blown-up balloon ready to pop" most of the time.

Amber's grades in school were marginal, school bored her completely, and she couldn't understand how her junior high school classes were going to help her support herself when she was on her own. She felt different from most of the other kids. She thought that adults didn't respect her, and she could immediately sense super-ficiality or hypocrisy in anyone around her, including her teachers and parents. When she respected a teacher, she would do the work to her own level of satisfaction; when she did not respect a teacher (most of them), she absolutely refused to do the homework and didn't care if she passed or failed. She hated being told she couldn't do something "because I told you so," or just because it had always been done in a certain way. She rebelled at what she considered to be rigidity, but longed for some benevolent structure that was geared to her as a "real person."

It was apparent to me by her awareness, her eyes, and her innate wisdom that here was a young adult with an expanded intelligence, definitely more mature than many of her peers, and in some ways, the adults surrounding her. She wanted to experience life on her own terms, yet she was a 13-year-old without the developmental maturity to make certain decisions for herself, and this annoyed her. She wanted to be an adult *now!* She loved to draw and feel the colors and shapes, move her body (dance), and most of all, she liked to experience life by "doing"—all characteristics of a kinesthetic learner.

Amber was extremely confused by the disparities in her environment. The life teachings of her parents, school, church, and what she observed in society were contradictory at times. To her, this was hypocritical. She felt contempt for adults who waffled around what she considered "truth." She loved feeling the rush of anger through her body and scaring everyone around her when she really let it out. Amber acknowledged that she was a bit of an actress and a tyrant, and she liked watching her parents and her brother tiptoe around her. She loved the drama, as it was the only time she felt powerful in the family. However, she knew she was close to going over the edge at times, and she was frightened that she wouldn't be able to stop herself. She also sensed that her parents didn't know what to do with her, and while she liked the feeling of power over them, deep inside she was afraid that hey wouldn't be able to protect her from herself.

Amber was very much loved by her parents, who had adopted her when she was an infant. Her brother, natural-born to her parents, was a few years younger. As a toddler, Amber was described as a "difficult" child, extremely self-willed and a little girl who "pushed the limits until she got what she wanted." As she grew older, she became more assertive and was quick to anger when her requests were denied. Her parents were truly perplexed and frustrated by her behavior, as their son was quiet, cooperative, got good grades, and participated in athletic activities. Amber disdained sports and thought that competition was "stupid."

Her family lived in a predominantly white, crime-free, middle-class neighborhood, with schools nearby. Both parents were educated and conservative. Amber's father was in middle management, and her mother worked part-time so she could be home with the children in the afternoons. Amber's parents encouraged both children to be active in soccer, baseball, dance, and other community activities. They attended church regularly. In other words, they were "good" parents.

When Amber came to me, I had recently been exposed to the work of Nancy Tappe and the Indigo Children paradigm. My intuition, and Nancy's description, told me that Amber was an Indigo, the first I had encountered as a professional. Very little of my training had prepared me for such an experience. I went with my gut and intuition most of the time, spoke to Amber as an adult, challenged her with love in my voice, and usually it worked.

Amber, a classic *humanist* Indigo, had the following characteristics:

- She wanted to love and respect her parents.

- She liked to be touched, hugged, and to be affectionate.

- She hated being alone—not out of fear, she just wanted to be around human companionship.

- She loved animals and they loved her.

- She lived in the moment, and when she knew what she wanted to do, she went after it.

- She expected honesty from the world around her, specifically her parents and other adults.

- She expected to be treated with respect, and when she wasn't, she reacted, sometimes violently.

- She knew she needed structure, not rigidity.

- She hated restrictions and wanted to make her own decisions.

- She absolutely could not be swayed or intimidated by guilt, and threats did not alter her behavior.

- She wanted choices, not mandates.

- She wanted to make her own mistakes, to learn from her "own experiences."

- She was bored in school and could see the weaknesses of the system and certain teachers.

- She liked right-brain, creative projects rather than linear, left-brain exercises, such as math and reading.

- She was extremely curious about everything, including death, drugs, and sex.

- She had an innate understanding of spirituality, and believed in an afterlife and reincarnation, which were not taught to her by her church or her parents.

- She did not like ambiguous adults and mistrusted secrecy.

- She could mentally erase another person from her mind if she felt they did not respect her, or were phony or insincere.

- She felt like an adult, yet she knew she was not.

- She could easily manipulate her parents
  with her temper tantrums.

- She was very intuitive and sometimes could
  read other people's thoughts.

- She was extremely sensitive to the energies
  around her, such as moods of other people.

- She felt no guilt about any of the above,
  and what she wanted most of all was to
  find her birth mother.

When Amber was 11 years old, she was snooping in her parents' office and found her adoption papers. For several years prior to that, she had asked her parents if she was adopted. They always told her, "Of course not!" When Amber related this story to me, her body shook, and she cried at what she considered to be the ultimate betrayal by her parents. How could they lie to her for so many years when she suspected they weren't telling her the truth? Why didn't they trust her with this information? Why was it such a big secret? Were they ashamed of her? Did they really think she would leave? Didn't they understand that she loved *them* and not her birth mother, whom she had never known? Did they think she was stupid? How could they not understand how awful it was to feel like she didn't belong to the family for as long as she could remember? Her rage, hurt, and feelings of humiliation were real.

Amber was teetering on the edge of her existence. She had thought of killing herself many times, had tried drugs, and was looking forward to the experience of sex. She needed and wanted guidance that she could trust, to be taught how to make choices for herself, and to find a constructive channel for her intense energy. She had obviously learned to manipulate her parents with her anger long before the adoption issue exploded, and she needed to learn to take responsibility for her behavior. The constant pressure of knowing she didn't fit in to her social and family environment just about drove her crazy. She was the round peg in a square hole, and she knew it.

As Amber was growing up, her parents felt like they were living with an atomic bomb. They had never been around a child like Amber, and they were at the end of their rope. As well intentioned as they were, they were not equipped to constructively handle an Indigo Child. Their only tools were their own family experiences and some reading in the popular press. The father was passive and withdrew into TV; the mother did most of the talking and disciplined the children.

There was very little hugging or touching in the family and seldom verbal "I love you's." As the emotional intensity in the family escalated, there was even less. Amber longed to be lovingly touched and spontaneously hugged by her parents, and to be reassured of their love. Both parents dutifully shuttled both children to and from activities. It was a typical family, busy *doing*, just like many other families in the neighborhood.

When I suggested to Amber's parents that they assist her in finding her birth mother, they were appalled. They feared that Amber would not return to them and they would lose her. I also suggested that they remove Amber from the public schools and place her in a performing arts high school, which would be more appropriate for her talents and orientation. This they also declined. Shortly thereafter, they stopped Amber's sessions with me and said they wanted a "second opinion."

A few years later, I ran into Amber's mother, who told me they finally did take my advice and moved Amber into another school environment that was more suited to her. Amber stayed in school and graduated. Her parents also helped her find her birth mother, which ultimately was a positive experience for the entire family. While they were still tested by Amber's behavior, her volatility and rage had lessened considerably after connecting with her birth mother.

I called Amber, and we had a wonderful telephone chat. She shared with me the details of her first encounter with her mother and her natural father, whose existence had been a mystery to her. Her birth mother and father had married a few years after Amber's adoption. Amber visited her birth parents every six months and never forgot to tell her adoptive parents she loved them and that they were her "real" parents. She told me that finding her blood parents helped give her a real sense of herself, and she didn't feel quite so different from other people. She also had a job, which fed her sense of self-sufficiency, and she was learning to take more responsibility for her behavior. Also, Amber's respect for her adoptive parents was restored.

Troubled Society, Troubled Indigos

Not all Indigo children are angry, volatile, and destructive. Some are so sweetly loving that they melt your heart. Indigo Children are unique individuals, just as all children are; however, as a group, they do have specific characteristics (see Amber's list), which are different from the children of previous generations. During the time Amber was in school, the percentage of

Indigo Children was much lower than it is today. Her feelings of being different from her peers were certainly exacerbated by the adoption issue; however, "feeling different" is a common complaint of Indigos. They know from an internal place that they see, feel, and respond differently to life than many of their peers and most adults. Today probably 95 to 100 percent of the children in the lower grades are Indigos; the maximum age range seems to be in the early 30s.

The percentage of troubled Indigos is in direct proportion to the number of troubled individuals, mothers, fathers, and families in our society. In this, the Indigo population is no different from previous generations. However, due to their sensitivity, they *feel* chaos, dysfunction, and the lack of nurturing love in their bodies and emotional fields much, much more than their predecessors. The resulting impact to their emotional development can be devastating, and it certainly accounts for an increase in drug usage (including so-called "legal" drugs such as Ritalin and Prozac), among children of all ages. Conversely, a supportive environment that encourages uniqueness, with benevolent boundaries, is likely to produce a balanced and incredibly interesting human being.

In addition to Amber, I know several Indigos who have had very troubled lives, and once they decided they wanted a different life, they quickly pulled themselves together. Indigos draw on enormous internal strength, can release addictions if they want to, and heal their lives with much more objectivity than most of us. Conversely, if they don't want to make any changes in their lives, *no one* can change their minds!

Suicide, Death, and Spirituality

The discussions I had with Amber, and subsequently with other young adults, made me wonder what kids really think about drugs, death, and spirituality. To find out, I put together a research protocol and invited young adults ages 16 to 19 to participate. I was amazed by their answers.

With the exception of a few details, answers to most of the questions were strikingly similar. The responses indicated deep, philosophical thought. Most of the participants' school grades were "average," with several "failing," and a few *A* students. Only one of the participants had formal religious schooling, one had been exposed to metaphysical concepts, and the remainder had some or no formal or parental religious exposure. Except for drug education classes, none of the participants had ever attended a class in school with discussions centering on death or spirituality, and parental instruction and discussion on these subjects was rare.

Regarding death: Most of the participants remembered *knowing* about death by the time they were five years old, some as young as three. They all believed that they came to this awareness without parental instruction or other influences.

The question was asked: "**What does death mean?**"

- "Stopping on the planet, but moving to something else."

- "Leaving the material body."

- "End of one part and moving to the next part."

- "Passing from one state to another."

- "Moving into another dimension."

- "The best thing about death is what's beyond."

- "You get to leave this planet."

They were *all* extremely curious about death and wanted to know how the actual experience of death feels. Over 75 percent had seriously considered suicide on more than one occasion, particularly those who were chronic drug users. However, of that group, 50 percent were not chronic drug users, but their lives were so painful that they didn't know how to stop the pain. (One participant wanted to "leave" when he was about five or six years old after his parents divorced.) Their love for their families, even if the family was chaotic, kept them from going through with the suicide attempt.

The next question was: **"Do you believe in a definite afterlife and an eternal soul?"** (Most answered "absolutely." A few weren't so sure, but upon reflection, they said that they did believe.)

- "You're born, you live, you move on."

- "I'm sure the soul goes on, I mean it's not the end, I know that."

- "Your soul inhabits a body, it borrows it from the earth, and then eventually it's going to have to give it back."

- "The soul goes out to wherever it goes, then I guess it stays there before it comes back into another body."

The last question was: **"What is it like to feel alone or feel different?"**

- "Alone means being without someone that's like me."

- "In a way, it makes me feel kinda sad and also proud that I'm a bit different from everyone else. Also sad, because I can't really bond with a lot of people. It's a trade-off."

- "It sucks."

At about the same time I completed this research project, I read the following article in *Family Circle* magazine (August 1991), which says it all.

A Lasting Legacy

In the mornings, 3-year-old Cody Thornton sits on the stairs chatting with the photograph of his big brother, Casey, that hangs on the wall. It was this spot that Casey [age 5] chose for a heart-to-heart talk with Cody in the fall of last year.

"Well, Cody," he said, "I'm dying, and that means I don't get to grow up with you anymore."

It had been two years since Casey was first diagnosed with acute lymphoblastic leukemia. The little boy had endured radiation, chemotherapy, an encouraging 14-month remission, two relapses, and a last-chance bone marrow transplant, and then another relapse.

"How hard do you want to fight this?" his mother, Julie, remembers asking Casey during this period.

His reply amazed her. He said, "Well, the five-year-old Casey wants to live really badly because I want to be with you, but I don't know what my soul is choosing."

Drugs and Indigo Angels

Drugs are an inescapable part of our culture. Americans *love* drugs! Our children are born into a society that spends billions of dollars each year for painkillers, anti-fat pills, decongestants, antidepressants, libido enhancers, birth control pills, and the list goes on. Add to that cigarettes and alcohol.

Sitting in front of me is Jenna, a pretty, 22-year-old Indigo with clear blue-gray eyes and a beautiful complexion. There is a sweetness about her.

Jenna was born into a family that consumed alcohol, cigarettes, antidepressants, and aspirin for hangovers. Not that the neighbors noticed, mind you. Jenna's father was a physician, and her mother was an artist.

Jenna can remember seeing angels and talking to the plants and birds at age three. She loved nature. She could look into the TV screen and see the universe and talk to the stars—she loved to look at the stars; they felt so familiar to her. At age seven, she announced to her parents that she didn't want to go to college and wanted to study the angels, stars, and E.T.'s. Her father said her thoughts were of "the devil and she was evil," and he punished her.

Jenna's mother took her to Catholic mass and she attended parochial school from grades three through eight. The only things she liked at church were the rituals, the incense, using a rosary, and singing. She didn't think it was fair that girls weren't allowed to participate in mass. She thought that the priests were "boring" and the nuns uncaring; no one spoke to Jenna's soul.

Jenna withdrew into daydreams and fairy fantasies. She liked to create fun outfits for school, and remembers the cruelty of the other children teasing her unmercifully in the sixth grade about looking "different."

There was continual tension in the home. Her mother was always depressed, and her father drank. One time she found alcohol hidden behind the toilet, and her parents had a violent argument over it. When Jenna did share her experiences with her family, she was ridiculed, ignored, or punished. One time her father locked her in her room and read Christian scripture to her while standing outside her door.

At school, Jenna felt alienated from the other students. She was quiet and felt invisible. When she transferred into high school, she automatically migrated to the kids with the dyed black hair, black clothes, and drugs. About this time, her father left the family. She remembers wanting to die; she was 13.

Shortly after her father left home, she took her first hit of acid. By 15, she was consuming alcohol, marijuana, and cigarettes; was hooked on speed, dropped out of school; and didn't care about anything. Jenna left home, lived where she could, and shoplifted to buy food and support her drug habit. By age 17, she was firmly addicted to heroin and cocaine, her drugs of choice. Her father continued to tell her she was "evil," and her mother tried to scare her into abstaining by telling her that "alcoholism runs in the family." By age 19, she had been in and out of seven treatment centers, felt hopeless, and was prepared to die. She was so ill that she hardly had the strength to get through each day.

During this time, she began to attend Alcoholic's Anonymous (AA) meetings. She was living in a "sober living" home. The turning point came when her roommate died from an overdose (OD), and another friend also OD'd and died the same week. The administrators of the home learned that Jenna had been using drugs during her stay, which was specifically against the rules. They asked her to leave, and within a few hours, she was homeless again. Her mother allowed her to return to her family home. The next day, Jenna was offered drugs and she declined; she was too sick. Without thinking too much about it, saying no was the beginning of her recovery.

Jenna was really angry with God. Her faith had been shredded little by little by the behavior of the adults around her. As a child, she noticed that grown-ups, particularly her father, did not walk their talk. If God was love, why was there so much pain in the world? If she was lovable and loved by God, why was there so much pain in her own life? She felt betrayed by her parents, the church, and God.

Jenna continued going to AA, liked the spiritual aspects of the program, and gradually began to function well enough to get a job. She wanted to lead a drug-free life. One evening she went with a friend to a recovery meeting (not AA) held specifically for young adults. Jenna resonated with the group, and particularly with Shannon, the facilitator, who wasn't too many years older than Jenna. From that time forward, Shannon became Jenna's mentor, one young adult mentoring another, both Indigos.

Jenna wanted to be what Shannon was: an open, confident, loving, fun, spiritually oriented young woman with a passion and a purpose in life. Shannon taught Jenna how to take care of her body, what foods to eat, helped her through detox, guided her in her choices, loved her unconditionally, and "didn't put up with any crap."

When Shannon created a live-in recovery home, she invited Jenna to live there and become a staff member, mentoring other young adults as Shannon had done with her. Jenna accepted. She has been continuing her own recovery process with Shannon, and she shares living space with the other young female staff members, all Indigos. She is employed full-time working with children in a day-care center, which she loves, and she donates the rest of her time to working with young people who are struggling with drugs and life. She has reunited with her father, who has been sober for several years, and she has a much closer relationship with her mother. Both parents give her encouragement and are proud of her.

Co-creative Indigos—Changing the World

I was introduced to Shannon about a year ago. She typifies the *Humanist* Indigo to the letter (see Amber's list), and then some. When Shannon was very young, she "knew" she would be working with troubled teens. She started working with kids when she was in high school and hasn't stopped. Her college degree is in sociology, with an emphasis on adolescent substance abuse. She is also a certified yoga instructor and massage therapist, and is trained in herbalism, nutrition, aromatherapy, and expressive arts therapy. She decided to create a recovery process and facility that would offer services designed to help young people change their self-destructive habits by focusing on physical health, emotional well-being, spiritual connection, and life purpose. And that is exactly what she's done, using her own paycheck to fund it. The organizational mission statement, prepared by Shannon and other Indigos, is as follows:

"Based on education and empowerment, the main purpose of the program is to assist youth, ages 15–25, in overcoming addictions, abuses, and disempowerment of their bodies, minds, and spirits. The program is three-dimensional, emphasizing the physical, emotional/mental, and spiritual aspects of healing.

"The program is founded on the premise that each of us has a unique purpose to fulfill, and that we're all interconnected. Therefore, what we do to our bodies we do to the larger Earth body, and inevitably, to each other. To address this, the program curriculum encompasses alternative health care, environmental awareness, life skills development, and spiritual growth.

"This is also a peer-based program. As a participant's sense of Self gains fortitude, they gradually become involved in peer counseling as a way of giving back, and helping guide other youth on their journey to Self-recovery. Young people function as volunteers, directors, staff, teachers, and peer counselors. This program exists as a vehicle for all youth to reclaim and rediscover their true Selves."

Shannon asked me to become a member of the organization's Board of Directors, and I accepted. Working with these young Indigo women has been a gift, and I marvel at them. Typical to the Indigo energy, they're determined to achieve what they set out to do, they're intense, are not intimidated by the scope of their mission, and they are totally dedicated to their spiritual growth.

The Indigos are here to stay. They are the rule-breakers that insist on change. They are the fresh air wafting over stagnant traditions, and they're the harbingers of a new society poised to shift into a more evolved consciousness. The Indigos' very existence challenges everything we do and say. They insist on sharp honesty and truth and will simply tune out and/or leave rather than fight if integrity isn't present in their environment. We can cooperate and grow with them, or resist and stay stuck in complacency. The choice is ours.

The needs of Indigos are simple: lots of love, benevolent structure, conscious guidance, and room to display their uniqueness. In return, our world will receive gifts we cannot imagine.

Peace

Hand in hand we walk
Together
Peace and I
And
All races
Black, white
And
All the
Whales waltzing in the sea
All the
Dolphins surging in the splash.
Hand in hand
We walk
Together
And wonder
Why war
Why anger
Why hate?
Peace and I
And all the
Creatures of the
Earth
Together forever
Walking hand and hand.
— *Sarah Barkley*, age 10

We'd like to close this chapter with an update on Ritalin. Many articles have appeared about this drug in the last two years—most of which were not positive. Dozens of Websites are dedicating themselves to presenting information on the long-term effects of Ritalin on kids, as well as offering assistance. It's a subject that has become mainstream.

We continue to encourage parents to try alternatives before deciding on the Ritalin route. Beyond the overwhelming information that's available on the biological ramifications of the drug, now there are psychological and cultural issues as well.

The following is an article from *Psychology Today* by Eben Carle (June 2000, p. 17):

ADHD for Sale

"On any given day in affluent Virginia Beach, nearly 20% of the young and privileged are on Ritalin, many of them needlessly," says pediatric psychologist Gretchen LeFever, Ph.D. Indeed, there has been an explosion of Ritalin use among children in the US, up from 900,000 users in 1990 to five million in 2000. Psychologists are pointing fingers at overly competitive parents, who will pay any price to secure advantages for their children.

LeFever's research, published in the *American Journal of Public Health*, found that while 3 percent to 5 percent of US elementary-school children have

Attention Deficit Hyperactivity Disorder, almost six times as many fifth-graders in Virginia Beach take medication for it, a number she says is typical in wealthy US communities. Parents turn to Ritalin, she explains, for its ability to stimulate concentration, forcing children chemically to "pay attention." But there's another advantage, says Yale professor Robert Sternberg. "Once kids are labeled learning disabled, there are so many benefits—extra help, extra time on tests such as the SAT—that people are fighting for the label."

Not surprisingly, many professionals are outraged. Late last year, members of the Center for Science in the Public Interest beseeched Secretary Donna Shalala of the US Dept. of Health and Human Services to intervene by encouraging the use of education- and discipline-based methods—rather than amphetamines—to correct behavior problems and motivate better performance. They also expressed concern with the side effects including stomach aches, insomnia and stunted growth, and with the discovery that Ritalin has caused cancerous liver tumors in laboratory mice. But this hasn't stopped parents. University of Colorado philosophy professor Claudia Mills, Ph.D., observes, "We give our children Ritalin in part because we cannot bear that they be below average; and we cannot bear that they not be above average."

Another pertinent article (Reuters News Service, September 14, 2000):

Lawsuits Assert Drug Makers and Shrinks Invented 'ADHD' To Sell Ritalin
by Edward Tobin
(entire article not shown)

NEW YORK (Reuters) — Richard Scruggs, the lawyer who led the settlement between U.S. states and the tobacco industry in 1998, called the lawsuits against the makers of hyperactivity disorder drug Ritalin the country's "next class-action battleground."

The Mississippi attorney heads up a group of plaintiffs' lawyers alleging in two lawsuits that the makers of the drug had conspired with psychiatrists to "create" the disease known as Attention Deficit Hyperactivity Disorder (ADHD).

Scruggs, who got his first taste of national class action suits with a successful run at the asbestos industry before tackling big tobacco, contends that the health of more than 4 million children is at stake because they are taking a drug that they do not need.

The two cases, filed in state court in Hackensack, N.J. and in San Diego federal court, name Swiss health care group Novartis AG (NOVZn.S), the American Psychiatric Association (APA), and a nonprofit support group called Children and Adults with Attention-Deficit/Hyperactivity Disorder (CHADD).

The suits seek class-action status and billions of dollars in damages. The allegations are denied by both the company and the APA.

"The main complaint is that they (the defendants) have inappropriately expanded the definition of ADHD to include 'normal' children so that they can promote and sell more drugs and treat more people," Scruggs told Reuters in a phone interview Thursday.

"These suits represent the latest class-action battleground in the U.S., but since it involves kids, this is that much more important. Government officials, pharmaceutical companies and medical professionals have debated over the prescribing of Ritalin for Attention Deficit Hyperactivity Disorder (ADHD) in children for some time. The drug has been on the market for over 40 years, but it came under intense pressure when the White House launched an initiative in the spring to cut down on the number of children using the treatment, known by the chemical name methylphenidate."

Scruggs, who tallied up $400 million in legal fees from the settlement with the tobacco industry, said public health was the main motivator in the Ritalin case, and the ultimate goal of the lawsuit is to change the way the drug is prescribed.

"Right now, virtually every child would fit the diagnostic criteria today for Ritalin. They are exploiting the fears of parents for the welfare of children to gain inappropriately, and I think that is very reprehensible and it can have a widespread affect on the health of American kids," he said.

The lawyers are seeking certification of a nationwide class, Scruggs said, and expect others will follow suit on basis that "the criteria for disease are artificially broad so that they can include more kids and sell more drugs."

"Nothing you do for children is ever wasted. They seem not to notice us, hovering, averting our eyes, and they seldom offer thanks, but what we do for them is never wasted."

— Garrison Keillor[1]

chapter seven

Through the Eyes of an Indigo

Some of the most profound responses to our first book were from teen and young adult Indigos. Although the "pure" Indigos are mostly children, many of their forerunners are teenagers and those in their early 20s. I don't think we have to spend much time alerting you, the reader, to how dramatic the teenage scene is becoming, or to some of the rage that we're seeing.

In *The Indigo Children,* we mentioned that one of the Indigo attributes is the feeling of being an adult in a growing body . . . that if the Indigos are not honored, they will indeed feel frustrated. They're almost grown, but they continue to be viewed as "children" by the educational system and their parents. The frustration at home has the potential to explode into other places (such as school, for instance), which gives us a good overall picture of the situation in our world right now.

In the first book, we printed two letters from young Indigos telling "what it's like to be an Indigo." The letters we received in response to these two stories were mostly from other young people, congratulating us and saying, "Me, too!" We'd like to present a few more Indigo stories from the perspective of young people. Although you might think this chapter is for *them*, it's really for *you*. The more we can listen to, relate to, and learn what our children and young adults are thinking about, the more we can bring peace to our families.

We didn't stack the deck here. Most of the letters we got started out, "I'm 16 years old." This seems to be a well-known demarcation point from childhood to the adult years, and it's a most critical time with respect to core life issues such as self-worth, romance, career choice, and so on.

Some of these letters came in right after we published the first book, and some just before press time on this second one. If we couldn't find the particular writer, we changed the name in the letter to honor the person's privacy. However, we don't believe they would object to letting you read their words; in fact, we think that's why we received the letters in the first place—in order to inform you about the Indigo phenomenon.

As you read this correspondence, remember that this information is raw, presented through the "filter" of young people who are in the throes of growing up (half-adult, half-child). They may not have all the answers, but they certainly do have the firsthand experience.

Remember some of the characteristics we cited in the first book? We told you that these children desperately need to find others of like mind. We also indicated a new feature of their temperament—that they did not want to be tested on things they already knew, or things they felt were below them. We also discussed the fact that teachers had to earn the respect of these children—and not just expect it simply by virtue of the fact that they're in positions of authority. We told you that some students could sense an imbalance in adults (teachers, in particular), and would turn themselves *off* to that individual. We also told you that if these children didn't get what they needed, they would form support groups of their own, or even seek outside stimuli that would enable them to vent their frustration and rage.

You're going to see some of these attributes in each story that follows, and also some common threads of discussion. Watch for something else: If a parent or teacher did a good job, the child will honor that. The child will also offer specific feedback on what they're *not* pleased with.

The last letter in this group is from an adult Indigo who wanted to tell his life story—to explain what it was like to question everything. He speaks of his personal evolution and his religious experiences as well. Remember what we told you about the spiritual Indigos? They like church, but it better make sense! They're very small shamanic creatures who can sense if the minister knows less than they do. (This often gets them in trouble.)

We want to honor each letter writer for their courage. We also want to honor their lives and let them know that we consider them to be valuable human beings. Their information is crucial to all of us, no matter how old we are. We've said it before: Some of these young people have much to teach us. I hope you "listen" as you read these heartfelt words from our youth.

To the Authors of *The Indigo Children*
Lisa Wallace

Even though I'm only on the first chapter of your book, I felt the need to write you. I'm 16 years old and know that I'm one of the children you're talking about.

I'm told that from a very early age, I began questioning where we came from. I would ask my mother questions she didn't even know existed. For the longest time, I felt alone, despite the fact that I had, and still do have, many friends and loved ones. I would often feel that

there was something more I had to offer than what every-one else had. More than once, I've been way beyond the maturity level for my age. I figured things out about the world, and myself, by the time I was a teenager, whereas my parents are still struggling with them today.

Throughout all of my life, I've felt incomplete and so very alone. Ironically, it wasn't until a few weeks ago that I discovered exactly where I stand on spiritual issues and my "other half."

Forgive me if the next thoughts are unclear, because I'm holding back information about what I want to say. During a conversation with one of my best friends, although he's always been more of a friend (not sexually, but spiritually), we discovered that we've both felt the same way. We've both been deeper than other kids, and have reached a level of acceptance in ourselves that some people never get to experience. We both feel—not bored at school, but—it just seems useless! We've also both felt so alone.

Through our conversations, we discovered that we're both old souls, and this is definitely our last life on Earth. After I hung up from talking to him on the phone, I realized that I was no longer alone. As I read about the other Indigos, I feel so connected with them. Would there be any way for all of us to meet, perhaps?

As I read your book, I get chills, and any moment I may begin to cry. It feels so good to know that there are others out there, for even though I've been surrounded by wonderful, glorious people, I felt completely isolated until I "met" my friend.

Now I know that the two of us aren't alone. Thank you for publishing your book.

My Life, Through My Indigo Eyes
Katarina Friedrich

I am an *interdimensional* Indigo child from Australia. I am 16 years old and recently went through what my mother calls my "midlife crisis." Three months ago, my mother, who has raised both me and my younger sister singlehandedly for more than ten years, was on the verge of taking me to a children's hospital to be sedated. I was screaming, crying hysterically, and pleading with her to let me go *home* (to let me die—return to Spirit). I was biting my arms and hands and quite literally tearing my hair out. I can remember begging her to listen to me. Someone, just listen!

My mother has always treated me like an adult and introduced me to all her friends as an equal. She has never failed to listen to me, always sensing when something was wrong and talking to me about it until I told her. So to be confronted with a teenager who was on the verge of insanity and begging to be heard was heartbreaking for her. Every time that she told me it would be all right, my screams doubled, since I knew that things were *not* all right and desperately wanted someone to help me. The real problem was not that my mother wasn't listening to me, but rather that the school wasn't.

My very early years of school were wonderful. I remember them largely in a dream of books, stories, storytelling, and magic. One of my most vivid and treasured memories is of lying under a tree laden with yellow blossoms, reading from a book—yet I'm not looking through my own eyes, but rather the eyes of something watching me. I only read stories halfway through, and I always gave them my own endings. I existed in a paradise that had little or nothing to do with teachers. I spent most of my time by myself, but I always felt content with this. I did feel very different from the people I was around, but I felt that this made me only different, not inferior or shunned. I watched others and observed how they acted, but didn't act with them. My favorite word was *Why?*, usually in the form of "Why did he do that?" or "Why should *I* do that?" These questions were not meant to be defiant or rebellious. I just wanted to know.

Around the age of seven or eight, things began to change. Music class was introduced into our school activities. Our lessons consisted of our teacher drawing musical notes on the board and getting us to bang them on tambourines in time with her, over and over and over again. I would stare at the tree outside the window and bash mechanically. After three weeks of this monotony, one particularly bright and alert seven-year-old boy jumped up and threw his plastic-skinned tambourine at the teacher's head. The scene that erupted was something out of *Lord of the Flies.*

This behavior quickly spread to all of the other students, and before long, any teacher who tried to control our class had no chance. If teachers yelled at us, the kids yelled louder. One teacher left on stress leave, and the next didn't bother to try and teach the class, but only to control them.

I spent most of my time at the back of the room doing schoolwork, which my mother had given me at home. At one point, I actually locked myself in the classroom, making it necessary for the principal to come and unlock the door. She took me to her office and yelled at me, to which I recall replying in a dead tone of voice, "Mrs. (teacher) is stupid and won't do anything."

My mother arranged to have me moved to another class, which had a very old, very strict, and very ugly teacher. I loved her! Admittedly, we all sat in rows and chanted multiplication tables, but she taught us how to embroider, and we made toffee apples for Christmas presents. Learning cursive writing meant that we would print a story in print and she would copy it in cursive. Then we would rewrite it, copying her impeccable script. She was a traditional teacher, but she was a *loving and caring* one, which is what she got back from her students. Unfortunately, she retired at the conclusion of that year, and I was back in the position I was in before. I refused to go back.

My mother was told by the school that I was only upset due to my parents' recent divorce. Concerned about this, my mother took me to a counselor who did a wonderful thing by telling Mum that she was a good mother and that the trauma I was under was due to school, not home.

My mother began to work through all the systems in order to try and change the situation within the school, but she was thwarted at every turn. In the end, she moved me to a different school.

Although didn't "fit in" at the new school, at least now I was receiving my ration of education—English, sciences, history, creative writing, etc. I excelled at them all, despite my early trouble in school. However, math was always, and continues to be, a difficult area. I find it frustratingly logical and stagnant.

I was the object of teasing, taunting, and ostracism at this new school, which hurt me deeply. I came to think of it as simply "part of these aliens' makeup." Teachers, however, at this heavenly place were wonderful! I had the opportunity to take writers' courses with professional adult writers, and through this, to meet one of my favorite authors, Christine Harris.

I sang in a choir, played the violin, and was also fortunate enough to meet another child like myself. Like me, he was shunned by the other students mainly because his topics of conversation were far beyond the intellect of most of them. Although we rarely spoke, for me the realization that there were other kids like me really meant a lot!

In high school, I was extremely lucky to be selected for a program that allows students to forge ahead in subjects that they excel at. I found this to be a blessing, as it allowed me to study additional units of history, social studies, biology, and the arts, while avoiding subjects that weren't relevant to me, such as math and the formula-based sciences. Also, I had the opportunity to manipulate my schedule so that I didn't have to be taught by teachers who I knew would hinder, rather than help, my education.

Then came my 16th birthday and the final year (so I thought) of school. Suddenly my ability to avoid superfluous assignments (because I already understood their content) was taken away. Every assignment had to be completed. It wasn't enough to be bright. I had to *prove* to these people that I was bright. I began to doubt that I was intelligent or valued. I became involved in my first sexual relationship with a man seven years my senior who made me feel valued and loved, but he had a very traumatized family and personal history of sexual, physical, alcohol and other substance abuse. This was a very draining relationship.

I left this relationship, a decision that was extremely painful, and felt completely alone. School was nothing but stress, and I had lost touch with the few friends that I'd made in my attempts to keep my relationship alive. My mother, who had always been my "Rock of Gibraltar," was in the beginning stages of her first serious relationship since her divorce ten years earlier, and was herself changing. I started eating badly and gained weight. This made me feel even worse. I felt ugly, shunned, unworthy, stupid, lazy, and guilty for being so depressed and horrible to the people I loved.

So, what got me to the stage where I can write this with only a few healthy tears? Love! I stayed with my father for a few days, and my paternal grandfather told me for the first time that he loved me. Then I stayed with my aunt for a few days. My maternal grandparents drove down from the country to be near me. My sister cuddled me, and my mother put her life on hold to see me through this time.

I went to a medical doctor who could do nothing, and admitted it. I went to a herbal doctor who gave me herbal preparations, which helped enormously, as did the use of the EMF Balancing Technique™. Finally, I received a message in a dream from a gnome who pleasantly haunts me.

The message said, "In the last lot, they had to try to change *themselves*. Your lot (the Indigo children) have got that already. You get to change the *world*."

To hear someone say that it is not about *me*, but the *world*, makes me feel better. I like the person I am, but I don't like everything in this world. I am okay. I am me. I can and will make a difference. The world will follow.

Many children today are accused of thinking that the world revolves around them. I hope that one day, it will.

I Know I'm an Indigo Child
Patty Doe

I am a 16-year-old girl who just finished reading your book on the Indigo Children. I believe I am an Indigo Child. Well, let's put it this way, I *know* I am an Indigo Child but have learned to phrase my statements to make them sound less ego-oriented to avoid negative feedback. That said, I'd like to thank you for your book and offer a few ideas of my own.

I really enjoyed the book. Not only was it a welcome affirmation, but it was also eye-opening in a few areas. I especially related to Candice Creelman's story (page 212 of *The Indigo Children*). Her stories of people showing jealousy and anger at her ease in learning is all too familiar.

The only part of the Indigo experience I did not relate to were the health issues, particularly ADD and ADHD. I am very fortunate to have had very supportive, accepting parents. They have raised me in an environment where I have been free to explore myself and my world. The spiritual aspects that you talk about in the book were seen as the norm in our house. I'm continually grateful for being raised in a home in which reincarnation and karma were the rules of life. I believe that it's because of this that I haven't faced some of the frustrations of not being understood.

My family and I have been trying to fight our way through the education system in our town for years now. I was blessed with aware teachers through grade school, but from sixth grade on, it has been a different story. I've seen many of my enlightened peers get frustrated and give up on the system. This has made me more determined to change it.

When I graduate next year, I would like to leave knowing that it may be a little easier for teens like me to get an education appropriate for them at my school.

The last issue I'd like to address is the feeling of isolation that many Indigos experience. I've always known that I was different. I'm not only an Indigo, but my mother owns a health-food store in a small community that is still suspicious of the alternatives she offers. We are not Christian, in an extremely Christian-based community.

Since my earliest interactions with other kids, I've known I was different, and I always felt grateful for this. I see others who don't understand me or what I'm about, but I don't look down on them. I have the knowledge that I have more awareness than they do and would not give that up for anything. I am the "weird" one and am content to be. I chose this life and am happy to accept the lessons it will give me and the path it takes me on.

I simply wanted to share these thoughts with you, to let you know that there are Indigos who are growing up and keeping hold of their intuition—Indigos who have not been overcome by their gifts and are using them for the good of others and themselves.

Thank you once again for the lovely book. I'd like to leave you with this little story. I have been blessed with meeting other kids like myself. Whenever I speak with them and we're describing another person to each other, we always get back to one question: "Are they one of us?" That's actually how we put it—one of us. That is always what we want to know about a person. Until now, I didn't think I consciously understood what "we" were. I simply knew that we existed.

Like Looking into a Mirror
Jacob Butler

I'm an Indigo Child who recently read your book, *The Indigo Children*. Wow! It was like looking into a mirror. I am an older Indigo. I'm 26 and am the father of two wonderful Indigo Children. I'm not having too much trouble raising them because I remember most of my childhood. A lot of the suggestions that are in the book, my wife and I are already using to encourage and guide them to be who they are. You'll have to excuse the jumpiness of my writing. I have so many things flying through my head that it's hard to get them all down in a truly coherent manner. I'll start with my growing up.

When I was little, I knew exactly who I was. I remember telling my parents about stuff—just things that I knew. But they would always tell me to just "be a kid." I didn't have a problem there, but I did know things. For a time while growing up, my brother and I slept in the loft above my father's wood shop. Our house only had two bedrooms, and my sisters got the other one. But it was cool. I used to come into my parents' bedroom at night and tell my mom about the flying saucers I could see. She told me that they didn't exist and to get back to bed. A few years later, I was sitting by my mother in church and told her I could see lights around people. I said I saw a red light around the painting of Jesus on the wall and wanted to know why he was mad. My mom told me that I couldn't see those things and that Jesus wasn't mad and to be quiet and respectful. After a few more instances like this, I quit telling people the weird stuff that I knew to be truth.

At the age of eight, my parents got a divorce, and my mother turned to New Age beliefs. This angered my father, who at the time was heavy into the Mormon religion. She moved away, and I only saw her about ten times after that. She kept in touch by letters and the phone and would relay all of her profound awakenings. I don't want to sound big-headed, but I just wanted to tell her, "Duh!" But I know that she had to go down her own path of awakening. She bounced back and forth from this to that, but she kept on her path fairly well. After my parents got divorced, my father got together with a lady who was also into New Age. She did provide some guidance in the way of meditation and made allowances for myself and my three siblings to be who we were . . . which carried over to my father when they split up. He always said that we were all so headstrong and he figured we would do what the hell we wanted to anyway, so he decided he would be there if we ever went too wild or fell too hard.

When I was a teenager, I really felt unwanted. All of the women my father had in his life either left or hated his kids. It was easy to blame myself. I had thought of committing suicide many times, but always stopped, knowing that there was something I was put here to do. I started remembering things from my youth that I had blocked out and also started meditating again. This helped some. I also started reading a lot of Eastern philosophy books. I really liked to read the book *Illusions*. I first read this when I was 12. But I remembered that when I was little, and I don't know if it was in a dream or what, but an elderly lady came up to me and asked me my name. I told her, "Jacob." Then she asked, "Ah yes, the healer. You have come here to be a healer of people and a teacher as well. When the time is right, your skills will be realized." Then she left with a kind smile.

I will be lying down, either resting or ready to sleep, when all of a sudden my body will freeze and I will be unable to move. I can't talk, breathe, or blink, but I'm still alive. I'm usually drawn to lights but not always. This used to scare me, and I would fight like mad to "get back to myself." But the last time it happened, and it hasn't happened since, I just let go of the fear, and there was a great pulling from my center *dan tien*, or *hara*, whichever you prefer. I felt like my whole body was being drawn up through my center. The vibration was incredible. Then there was a flash of light, and what I became next was unexplainable. I became everything. I was a part of everything, and everything was part of me. The emotion and the overwhelming sense of love and belonging were more than words can say.

After this, I fell into a deep sleep and woke up the next day completely disoriented. I had to be alone to process what had happened. I was afraid to tell anyone out of fear of the old persecution. But I told my wife, and she let me know it was okay. I wasn't going crazy. I also told my Tai Chi teacher, but he didn't understand. It was such a vivid experience that I remember it like it was yesterday. I have also had many dreams that have helped me realize my true nature, as well as that of my children.

About three months after my son Dylan (son of the sea) Elihu (guardian angel) was born, I had a dream. He was about the age he is now, eight, and big for his age, as he is in real life. We were at his birthday party, and the other kids were playing. He sat down beside me and started having an adult conversation with me about life and why we're here—after which, his sister Jaiden (royal stone from China) Samantha (fire) sat down, and started to listen. He said that one day I would wake up and realize who and what I was. He said that my real name was Tamalar. He also said that he was from Cetus and was sent here to be a teacher of man, as have others. He told

204

me his mother's real name, but I couldn't remember it when I woke up. He said we were also from the same place he was.

This was more than eight years ago. It was such a powerful dream that I called my mother and told her about it. She wrote it down, and I'm grateful that she did because I had all but forgotten about it until recently. When she sent a letter to Dylan telling him about it, he read it, and I asked him what he thought. He just said, "Cool. I like it." Then he went off to play. He and his sister have at times astonished my wife and me with their comments and remarks that are so wise and profound for their age. But then when I remember who they are, I'm not so surprised.

While I was growing up, my father had us kids in the Mormon religion until the age of eight. When I was young, I enjoyed going to church, but then as I grew up, I started to question some of the beliefs that I was being presented with. It wasn't that I didn't believe in God, or the Prime Creator, but I wanted to find out where other beliefs were, and why we did some things that had nothing to do with God. When we were with my first stepmom, my dad had us go to a Unitarian church for a while. It was all the same thing, just under a different name. Then we went to a Lutheran church for a while—still no change. But they all claimed to be the *true* religion. I believe the true religion is within. That's where we will find God and truth, not in a church, a place, or a statue. Sure, it's nice to get together with others and discuss experiences or work through tough times, but I saw through all of it and felt many were afraid to look within. I hated my dad for making me go.

After he and my stepmother split up, we did not go to church for a while. We moved in with my grandparents, and then Dad started getting back into the Mormon church. There he met my current stepmom, a lady I love and cherish. She is also Mormon, but allows us to believe what we want, and knows we are all good kids.

When I turned 12, my father pushed me to join the priesthood of the church, and I flat-out refused. He allowed me to hold fast in my decision, although he got a lot of flack from others in the church. I was also "causing problems" in Sunday school because I was asking questions. How dare someone do that! I guess that was somewhat like my school setting. I was kind of a troublemaker. I would not pay attention and distract other kids, but when I was asked questions about something, I could always answer and turn the question around to the teacher, who quite often had trouble with the answers. I got kicked out of Sunday school for a while and had to go through counseling with my grandpa, who is high up in the priesthood. I told him that all I was doing was asking questions. It wasn't my fault the teacher couldn't answer.

Through all of this, I was reading Eastern philosophy. I also got kicked out of the special class for teenagers that the church has where they do advanced Bible studies to prepare for their missions, called *seminary*. My father was the teacher at the time, and we were talking about Jesus. I kept chiming in with comments about Buddha and how he was born 500 years before Christ and how similar their teachings were. He didn't like this at all and said I didn't have to attend anymore.

Later in life, I discovered that we should read through all the teachings, take what is relevant to our unique situations, and like the Buddha taught, find the middle path. Everything we do should be out of kindness and love. I know in my life I've never done a thing for anyone expecting anything in return. No matter how large the favor, a simple thank you is compensation enough. I don't know how to get people to realize this. When I talk to others about it, they don't listen because I'm young.

I know that I'm a healer and a teacher, but people won't listen to me. Why should I talk? I know that what I have to say is important, but I don't know if people are ready to hear it. When I do get a chance to get into a discussion, others dismiss what I have to say. For example, when I told my Tai Chi teacher about the Indigo Children book, he said it was a bunch of New Age crap, and that was it. I did get him to admit that spiritual and psychological evolution is possible, but he doesn't think it can happen right now. I told him whether it is or not, we have to hope. Without hope, nothing would change. If nothing is going to change in our world, I don't see the point in continuing this existence. I hope he heard me.

When I graduated from high school, I got married. My wife and I moved to Hawaii and lived there for a while, then moved to Colorado, where we are today. My wife has successfully rebuilt a relationship with her father and is working with her mother. I believe that she is also an Indigo Child. That's why I felt so comfortable with her and felt like I could tell her anything from the day we met. We've been married for nine years and are happier than ever.

I'm writing this letter to you to see if you have had any communications with other Indigo Children who feel as frustrated as I do. We know who we are and we know why we're here, but it seems that many others aren't ready for us. I was wondering if there would be a possibility of arranging a meeting of Indigos of all ages, especially the older ones. It would be nice to talk to people who have had similar experiences and understand what I'm still going through. I feel like I'm at the top of the hill. I've reached the summit, and I'm ready for things to start rolling, but how? How do I fully realize my talents and put them into application? The world needs to realize that we don't have to live like this. We can all have what we need, and there will be plenty for everyone. We just need to live in light and let love rule.

chapter eight

What We've Learned

"In all our efforts to provide "advantages,"
we have actually produced the busiest, most competitive,
highly pressured and over-organized generation of youngsters
in our history—and possibly the unhappiest.
We seem hell-bent on eliminating much of childhood."

— **Eda J. Le Shan**, U.S. educator, and author of
The Conspiracy Against Childhood[1]

It has been two years since the original Indigo information was released. In that period of time, we've seen some of the basic information we originally presented about Indigos become front-page news. We spoke emphatically about how some of the primary educational tests were obsolete, and how children were reacting to them. As we write this book, the cover of *Time* magazine (March 12, 2001) features the Scholastic Aptitude Test (SAT), with articles and discussions from educators suggesting that this test, originally developed in 1926, is indeed obsolete and should be scrapped.

Teacher-assisted cheating, failing schools, a national program for school vouchers, home schooling, and an amazing group of ADD- and ADHD-related news stories have been prominently featured in the national press and television shows. As we've mentioned, scandals involving Ritalin have also become headline news, and the suggestion that some children are now using illegally acquired Ritalin as their "drug of choice" seems to validate our original warning that this drug is usually not an answer, but simply a Band-Aid—and a poor one. Now we're actually facing the possibility of widespread addiction!

On the positive side, a full-page article in *Time* showed six-year-old children practicing yoga, as we earlier indicated, with the suggestion that children "take" to these types of inward-introspection activities better than anyone would have imagined. Many other magazines have also run articles on the "new kids," (not necessarily calling them Indigos).

There are also summer camps for Indigos springing up around the country, as we indicated earlier. Want to see one in Idaho? Go to the Internet and visit **www.campindigo.org**. Here is a quote from the site: "The camp encourages each child to explore his or her own truths, talents, and abilities; teaching them respect for themselves, others, and the environment."

Then there are the kids who kill other kids. We've never had a more "in-your-face" attention-getter than this. These tragedies are profound wake-up calls, demanding basic changes in parenting and schooling—something that represents the foundation of our work, and has for many years. Our hearts pour out to these parents and students who have been part of these horrific episodes. It seems that the unimaginable is happening over and over to these precious souls we call our children.

Anger is at a high level, mostly due to the frustration of a generation of parents and educators who feel that they've done their best, but that something has "slipped between the cracks" to allow such a fundamental flaw to develop in mainstream schooling and education—a flaw that warps the mind of a child who would take a gun to school to execute other kids.

We received letters from some very concerned and highly educated professionals who wrote us that it was unconscionable that we would make our second Indigo book one that was "warm and fuzzy." They told us that there wasn't anything warm and fuzzy about what was happening. They needed help and felt that this second book should be similar to the first—that is, providing advice for parents and educators. In honor of their concerns, we'd like to say that there are books in progress from other authors (as well as ourselves), which will indeed pick up this gauntlet and provide additional academic information.

One of these new books has been written by an original contributor of our *Indigo Children* book, Doreen Virtue, Ph.D. She has written *The Care and Feeding of Indigo Children*,[9] published by Hay House (the publisher of this book) in August 2001. More works are on the way, and the term we introduced in 1999, "Indigo Children," is now being used all over the Internet as well. A recent search for the words *Indigo Children* on one of the top search engines of the Internet (a tool that scans the World Wide Web for subjects), brought up more than 68,000 responses.

As we write this book, two memorial services and funerals are being held in our own community of San Diego. Photos of the two high school students shot and killed in the Santana High School incident in Santee only a week ago are posted all over the community. There is considerable anger and frustration. Parents are blocking the streets, honking in protest at the myriad national press trucks that are invading our town like electronic vultures as they rudely thrust microphones and cameras in the faces of grieving parents, teachers, and students. *"How did it feel? What did you see?"* The public is tired of reliving this horror. We want answers, not more reality TV.

On March 10, 2001, Bill Maher, host of the TV program *Politically Incorrect,* took his place in front of the camera and told a national audience how angry he was. He said it was time to "take back our families." He said that making children partners in the family was wrong. "They were taking over," he said, and "were controlling our lives." He went on to say that children should do as they're told, the way they did in his day, and not be given equal status. They should be put in their place. Adults were wise, and kids were not, he indicated, and we shouldn't let them "run us" anymore. He was serious! We sat in front of our televisions and felt betrayed by the ignorance inherent in these old ways of thinking.

No school shootings have been attempted by children who have been honored in the family, who have had "best friends" as parents, and who have been given choices as "partners in the family" while growing up. These very basic Indigo parenting attributes give children self-esteem, and the ability to discern between right and wrong when they're subjected to the peer pressure that is inevitable in our society.

Almost without exception, the school shootings have been perpetrated by confused children who have not had the ability to discuss their problems at home, or who had parents who were so oblivious to what their kids were doing that bombs were being built in their very garages without them knowing it! The record shows that the "killer kids" were mostly frustrated, often bullied at school, and unable to cope with day-to-day stressors. Instead of being able to come home to a "friend" within the family structure, some of these kids created a "rageful" reality of their own with death games and hateful Websites. Research now shows that some of these kids were even on Ritalin, again indicating to us that this drug doesn't do everything promised. These children didn't communicate with their parents or perhaps didn't feel close enough to anyone in the family to be able to initiate a dialogue.

With all due respect to Mr. Maher, a fine comedian, we feel that he did a disservice to children everywhere by his comments. Do we really feel that any of these kids, now either dead or in prison for their acts, would have behaved far better had we slapped them down early on and told them to "behave or else?" These are Indigos—wise humanity in small bodies, being forced into a paradigm that is absolutely devastating to some of them. If they're full of rage, you can blame the restrictive situations they were put in—those characterized by high walls of indifference, or grown-ups too busy to stop and share.

We continue to believe that the core answer to the phenomenon before us is a basic change in attitude with respect to raising children. Make them partners in the family. We never suggested that they should be dictators or take over. Giving children choice and respect in the family isn't putting them in charge. Discipline is still needed, and "drawing the line" as to what is acceptable is still a valid component of parenting. What happens, however, when you honor a child while they're growing up, is that family discipline is much better understood and accepted than with a child who is simply told, "Wait until you're older," "You don't know anything at your age," or "Do what I tell you."

To follow the advice of Mr. Maher would be to return to the ways of parenting that were common 50 years ago. This, by the way, is an opinion shared by many who continue to throw up their hands in frustration. They feel that since *they* "turned out okay," why not go back to "the good ol' days" when kids were seen and not heard, respectful to their parents, and not shooting up schools. If this were the case, how do you explain the recent explosion of child violence in Japan? Here is a culture renowned for the attributes of the child-parent relationship. The Japanese have always seemed to give us a wonderful cultural model for the family unit. Their children are well behaved and honor their elders. Recent news coming out of Japan, however, points to the fact that some of the very problems we're having in America are also prevalent in the Far East. Here's an excerpt from a *Time* magazine article (January 8, 2000).

Japan's Wild Ones
by Tim Larimer

During the country's [Japan] lost decade of economic stagnation, real-life youth have been on a steady, descending spiral of listlessness, disenchantment and rebellion. . . . With increasing frequency, young Japanese began erupting in unexplained fits of rage. Violent crime rates among youths are way up (increasing by nearly 25% in the first 11 months of 2000) from a year earlier, as are student dropouts and crimes committed at schools. A recent government survey found that about one-quarter of junior-high students admitted they sometimes "explode with anger or resort to violence." Last year alone, Japanese teenagers were responsible for: a bus hijacking in which a passenger had her throat slit; the baseball-bat murder by a young man of his own mother; and the fatal stabbings of a family of three. And just last month, a 17-year-old boy fashioned a bomb out of nails, screws, gunpowder and a coffee cup and set it off in a Tokyo video store. He was carrying a shotgun and told police, according to the local papers: "I wanted to destroy people." . . . Something clearly is happening to Japanese youth. If animation, video games and movies aren't to blame, what is?

Our information tells us that children have changed, and that no old model, no matter how well it used to work, is going to work now. The '50s and '60s are now gone, and with them, an old culture of innocence has passed, as well as a world with half as many people. The Indigos are a product of human evolution, and they offer hope to all of us. Against all odds, humanity seems to have bypassed all of the millennium prophecies and Armageddon doomsday scenarios. Instead, we now stand at a crossroads of consciousness where our children are informed, wise, and are primed for a different kind of parenting and schooling. They face a world where tolerance is beginning to show itself in brand new ways, and where old paradigms of politics and religion are starting to look like shams to them. Integrity is often number one on their humanity radar, and when they don't see it, even at a young age, they react. Sometimes when they don't find it at home or at school, they retreat, turning inward as they attempt to discover what else the world may offer, or better yet, what they might create themselves through their anger and rage that might work better.

Some young people, who are as frustrated as we are, want to communicate what *their* ideas are on this subject, also. After all, they're living it! Sometimes we think that young people are in a vacuum, and that only we as adults can meet, have committees, write books, and solve this dilemma. But more and more, teens and young adults are gathering by themselves, driven by their own sense of responsibility, and yes—even writing books. Here is one we highly recommend, written by a very young man. It's called *Can Students End School Violence?: Solutions from America's Youth*,[10] by Jason Ryan Dorsey. This is what Amazon.com has to say regarding Jason's book:

> Compiled by America's foremost young speaker, twenty-year-old Jason R. Dorsey, each section is packed with youthful insight and action-oriented solutions. Working with over 150,000 youth from every background across America, Jason deals directly with their

experiences, challenges, and opportunities daily. To help our youth, we must learn directly from them. We must shape our schools from the inside-out, students first, because they are the ones that create and suffer from school violence.

You might have noticed that none of our writings present problems without solutions. We try to feature books that identify certain issues and also give suggestions on what to do.

So, given that statement, we offer you the following. Your success with respect to parenting an Indigo, or near-Indigo, depends on several conditions:

1. *Your child's age.* How much time has passed without realization of their Indigo attributes?

2. *Where you live.* Let's face it. Some of you live in areas where survival is far more important than anything else. It's tough to relate to some of these higher-minded things when putting food on the table is your biggest concern

3. *Your situation.* Single parent? Inadequate school district?

4. *Your courage.* Often the hardest thing to do is to open up a dialogue with your own kids. We know this is true.

Let's look at each of these items in more detail.

— *Age:* If you have a toddler and you're reading this, then you're fortunate. You have the ability to begin parenting in a new paradigm. You get to truly discover your child, and revel in their acceptance of things that are new and very "Indigo-like."

Many of you, however, have children who are older. They are preteen or teen, and some have already decided that you are only one step above dog poop. They roll their eyes every time you talk to them, shuffle their feet and stare at the floor instead of looking you straight in the eyes, and communicate the unspoken body language of "Yeah, whatever." Then when they're finished with their non-listening session, they're out the door to a private life you only hope is something you would approve of.

It's time for the interaction of a lifetime—a forced meeting where you drop your shield and hope it's not too late. Chances are it won't be. Inform your children that you want to talk. Ask *them* to choose a good time. Tell them you'll need an hour. Demand that they set a time for this, and then don't let anything disrupt this schedule—not anything. Right away, you're showing your kids that this meeting is more important than any other errand or family matter. Be prepared for the possibility that they'll protest strongly (putting it mildly). But insist.

Sit down in front of them with a notepad, and ask them to look at you while you talk. Start by telling them that this is not a lecture where they're going to be disciplined, talked down to, or berated. Tell them that more than anything else in the world, you want to be their a friend. Then ask them to tell you what isn't working for them.

Posture yourself for openness. Don't expect a miracle, but above all else, be unconditional in your acceptance. Remember, this meeting is about *them,* not you, so don't tell them how it was when you were a kid. Don't lecture. Don't get mad. Don't flinch when they tell you things that are blatantly wrong or exaggerated or even hurtful. Remember, if they really open up, you're hearing life straight from the horse's mouth, right or wrong. Let them rant about you. Let them complain about everything, even if it's not fair for them to. Take notes. It shows you care. *Listen* . . . just listen.

In the end, don't do the expected thing. Don't retaliate point by point. Not yet, anyway. Understand that most of what was presented stems from what they're *feeling*, which is the whole point of the meeting. Get creative. Ask them to elaborate on what's important to *them*—something you might be able to help with. Perhaps they feel you're too strict; too old to understand their music; not appreciative of their fashions or their friends; or not loving, caring, or smart enough.

This first meeting should end with a set of questions. Each case is different, but here is a sample of what you might ask:

1. *"What can I do to improve your life?"* They may respond by stating things that are absurd or way off base. It doesn't matter. You're creating a catharsis for your children—a safe place—and it also allows them to vent. You're also starting to develop a new and fresh bond that wasn't there before. Swallow hard and *listen*. Remember, just because you're listening doesn't mean you're going to do everything they're asking for.

2. *"Are there some compromises that we can work out? What would you do if you were me?"* This is thought-provoking and also tells your kids that you're serious. They may actually have a chance to make their lives better, so they may take advantage of this opportunity. Since you're not in a vacuum (hopefully), some of the areas of discussion won't shock you. So be prepared with some compromises, and start negotiating important issues.

Be ready to *give* something. Try to remember how you were in your youth, and put yourself in your kids' place.

3. *"Is it too late for us to be friends? Will you promise to come to me if you need help? Will you meet with me again like this?"* These are the big questions, and they represent the primary reason for this initial talk. Your kids may give lip service to these questions but not be ready yet to answer truthfully. The reason? They don't trust you! This is hard for any parent to hear, but it's true. Many preteens and teens are far more trusting of someone they've known less than a year who is their own age, than the parent who gave birth to them.

A number of these special meetings may be needed, and the children will eventually get used to the fact that:

- the meetings don't turn into fights. (This has to be a promise you make to yourself, and it will take wisdom and great self-restraint on your part. If fights do occur, even once, then you have effectively undermined this entire process. We told you it wouldn't be easy. . . .)

- you don't blast them.

- they can actually talk to you without everything blowing up. Just be present and listen to their *feelings*. Don't ever define them during these times. This is not a time for lectures, or even adult wisdom. It's time to sit and *listen*.

Eventually, according to what many parents have told us, you will be able to talk about school, their friends, their music, and many other topics that you may slowly draw out of them or that are revealed . . . yep, even sex. The result? Your kids acquire a friend called Mom or Dad. Some parents even go the extra mile. They'll attend a concert with their kids, go shopping for clothes, and so on. It might not be what *you* personally want to do, but your children will never forget it—ever. Is it worth the effort? Yes! After all . . . don't you want your children back?!

— *Where you live:* You might live in an affluent neighborhood or a ghetto. The school your child attends might be an honors school or one where there's a daily weapons check. One of the interesting things to note is that most of the widely publicized school killings were *not* in ghetto schools, but instead represented upper-middle-class neighborhoods. The ghetto children tell us that they have killings too—just not as dramatic—and the events don't make the evening news.

Each situation is different. The chances are that families who are in survival mode are more apt to communicate better with their children. The kids are engaged in tasks and responsibilities very early in life, and therefore have a better opportunity to dialogue with their parents. Even in this situation, however, the procedures listed above are still needed at some point. Eventually, some of the big questions have to be asked to make kids understand that no matter what your situation, their input is needed.

— *Your situation:* Are you a single parent? That means that you don't have as much help. It also means that your situation is common to many others in your same situation, so it's not unique. You can still make this work with small children or a teenager. It simply means that the approach must be slightly different. You might need to request additional help on their part to make it work. Questions can be asked such as: *"Do you know why we're alone?"*

Without bashing the mate that may have left (since quite often the children visit him or her), try to openly discuss what happened in simple terms. The loss of love, addiction to substances, infidelity, and many other seemingly adult subjects may be openly discussed in simple ways. You might be very surprised by how much a child does understand. It will also bond the two of you. Don't make the other partner "wrong." Explain to the youngster how you feel about what happened, not who did what to whom.

If a mate has died, then carefully talk about death in general. It's real and "in your face." You can't ignore it and just hope that someday your kids will understand everything when they're grown. Speaking about death takes away much of the misunderstanding and fear. Not speaking openly about the death of someone close to you often creates a situation where your kids may think it (death) is so bad and so dark that it might come for them in their sleep any day (or worse, that somehow they were responsible).

Discuss how much you miss the departed mate and how it feels to you. If the mate was lost when your kids were old enough to be aware, then be open to grieving together. We have heard reports that some very small children have heard a mother speak of how it felt, and they hugged and hugged the mother—telling her it would be "okay." They actually went into "nurse" or "mother" mode. This is a real friend. End the conversation by promising to make things better, and decide what that might mean. You've just created what we like to call the "joy team."

Do you have a school that is giving you or your child problems? Are they using an old paradigm of teaching and can't see what is really happening with your child? What can you do? Repeated meetings with teachers and counselors can only go so far. Some schools (we are told) will eventually list you as a "difficult parent" if you hang out in their offices enough. What can you do?

The answer, of course, is to try and transfer your kids to better schools or institute home schooling. The reality, however, is that this is not always possible. The law, your financial situation, where you live, and so on, often prohibits this. Many parents have told us that the answer (again) is a meeting of the minds between you and your child. Become their "homeroom." Commiserate with them when things don't go well with a teacher or with some bully at school. Let them always know that they have an understanding conduit in you, and that although neither of you might be able to change the situation, you can both laugh or cry about it together. Set aside a time to talk, then do a lot of listening. Don't let a busy schedule simply wipe out the opportunity. You'll be amazed what this will accomplish. It often disarms the situation, or better still, gives your kids courage for the next day. Then everyone feels bolstered and ready for tomorrow. Think about it.

— *Your courage:* Why is this so hard? One reason is that these kids have spent their lives with you. They really know you! They know what you look like in your underwear, and how you look in the morning even before the mirror sees you. All your addictions, bad habits, and mistakes are right out there. This makes it tough to talk, or communicate in any fashion. Sometimes the older children act more like unwilling roommates in a prison than loving family members.

But you remember what happened after the teenage years, don't you? You woke up one day and wondered how your parents suddenly got their "smarts" or when they calmed down? They didn't change—*you* did! You were probably about 23 or 24. In other words, there *is* hope, and often growing up naturally tears down the walls that existed during those awkward times. But waiting is not an option. Many parents have reported that the so-called generation gap was closed up to a great extent via the techniques we've listed here, and that getting their kids to trust them was the best gift the universe ever gave them. It was a win-win situation, where the benefits were clear to everyone.

I guess this is to say, as authors on this subject, that we know it's difficult, and we salute your courage as you evolve alongside these new Indigos. To make this procedure more palatable, we will report what some parents have told us:

Never lie. As we've mentioned, Indigos are extremely intuitive. They can tell if you're not giving it to them straight, and distinct chasm is created between you if you aren't. Even a half-truth that parents tell their children to shield them from harsh reality isn't a very good idea anymore. Can't pay the rent? Worried? Don't share your fears, but go ahead and tell the truth if your kids want to know something. Then follow up with some kind of positive, reassuring message for both of you: *"We'll work it out—we're a good team. This, too, shall pass."* (Or words to that effect.) Your kids are better off knowing why *you* are upset, rather than wondering if it was something they did to cause it. The truth is always best. Try to posture it with integrity and honesty, and your kids will understand. If there's a crisis, then pray with them! Include them as much as possible—not in your fear process—but in your reality and in your hope for a solution.

Inform them about important family matters before final decisions are made. Although in reality, kids may not be able to influence major decisions (for example, if you and your spouse need to move), but by including them in the discussion, they'll feel that they're not just being pushed and pulled by circumstances. If they're privy to your decision processes, they'll be more likely to accept the situation without blowing up. You also might get insight into any fears they have with respect to certain situations, prompting you to take action that you might not otherwise. What's the result: Your kids will remember all their lives that their parents trusted them enough to include them in this way.

Try to understand what gives your kids joy, and then ask them if you can occasionally participate in some activities of theirs. Perhaps your children engage in a hobby that you think is stupid, unproductive, or juvenile. Think back to when you were a kid, and create some tolerance here. Go with them to places where their interests lie—even if there's nothing there for you. If you don't understand anything about it, just tell them so, but be open to explanation. Skateboarding contests . . . strange fashions . . . offensive (to you) music . . . inane comic book conventions . . . vegan restaurants . . . extreme sports . . . tractor pulls (oops, sorry . . . that's a husband thing) . . . anyway, you get the idea. Try to get involved with your kids without violating the "Don't bring a parent" rule. This means that there are some activities that you absolutely must not be a part of—and they'll let you know what these things are rather than suffer the ridicule of their friends. Ask them, *"Is this something you would rather do with your friends?"* They'll always tell you.

Also, barter with your kids. Take them somewhere they couldn't go without your driving them, paying for them, et cetera, and in return, ask them to go somewhere with you—perhaps a play, a quality movie, or a symphony concert. When you both give a little, a partnership of sorts is established.

Discipline: Use it sparingly, and make it clear what your boundaries are. Try to make sure that the rules of the family are commensurate with the times, and are not necessarily what you were subject to when you were growing up. Times change, so make certain you know all the fact before you automatically say no to something that might now be acceptable to society—and even to most other parents.

The lines you draw and the expectations you have with respect to meals, TV viewing, curfews, computers, games, and dress codes will be much more acceptable if you and your kids talk about them face-to-face. Again, some bargaining with your child might be a good idea, and might help them understand that you're reasonable and trying your best to make things work for everyone. Don't just post the rules—discuss them!

In the end, however, *you* are the parent, so if you have to make a choice that your kids don't like, let them know *why* you made that decision, then stick to it. After all, adults face this type of situation in their lives all the time. You might remember what it was like at work if you were ever demoted, criticized, or fired (gulp). To some degree, these are the same emotions that your kids feel when they lose a bargaining point or don't get their way. Respect their feelings, and try to balance discipline and rules with love.

To put it simply, growing up ain't easy, but having loving, understanding, and fair parents will always bring reason and logic to any interaction, dispute, or discussion. Discipline used to be "Do it or else. Do it because I said so." Now it's "Do it because you're in a family where we work together" or "Do it because we respect each other."

The U.S. is founded on majority rule and minority rights. You might have to point out the way an entire nation has been able to live together for 225 years, and the beauty of a system where not everyone always gets their way. *You* are the majority, and your kids represent the minority. You may win, but they have rights, too.

Touch your kids often. Yep—even the teenagers. This actually helps them *get back into* their bodies. Dads, do it enough when they're young, and they won't back off nearly as much later. Even the boys will accept a hug from you. If you never did it before, then start. Let them push you away the first few times. Do it anyway. They will eventually accept it. And they might even give it back—eventually!

The experience of raising children is perhaps the greatest test of any human being. It is also the greatest reward. There are many paths and many outcomes, many stories and many reactions. Sometimes things don't always turn out the way we wish, but as you face this enormous challenge, the question is: How will you handle it? With love, compassion, and reason . . . or with dissension and ill will? The choice is yours.

Many of you reading this book have lost children through death or illness, so to pay homage to those who are gone, and to especially honor the potential of those who remain, we want to present a final story by Betsie Poinsett.

Mothers Who Cry in the Night
Betsie Poinsett

Thank you for addressing these precious souls who blazed the path for the new Indigos. You got my attention right away, as I had been thinking about them when I read Lee's post on the Internet asking us for stories about the Indigo Children. I went to sleep thinking about it and woke this morning knowing I had to write.

My son was one of the pre-Indigos. I can say that he gave his life for the cause. He died at age 21 in1997, never wanting to be in this 3-D world, and yet transforming everyone he came in contact with. His Indian totem was the Dragonfly—shifting everyone between the dimensions. His behavior here (drugs, drinking, DUIs) stretched me to every limit. He had many accidents, walking away from many without a scratch, until the last one. Then "poof!"—he was gone. My test was to either transform spiritually or crumble. I chose transformation.

After my son died, people would call to tell us how spiritual he was and how he had transformed their lives. My husband and I would just look at each other and wonder if they were talking about the same person. He had pushed us away from the time he was about five. I think it was because he knew he wouldn't be here long. After he died, he was right here with me, like an electric sizzling energy, giving me messages and appearing to many people. I realized then that in the "big picture," he had been here as a master teacher.

He left behind more than 200 poems and songs that we never knew he had written! I'm trying to get them in book form now in his memory, plus I'm writing a book about my experiences with him called *Mothers Who Cry in the Night.*

One of his friends has had more than 20 friends die in the last four years. Do you have any idea how many of these kids have come and gone? I can think of more than 35 off the top of my head. They *do* need to be honored. Without them, these new Indigo Children wouldn't be possible. Here's part of a poem that my son wrote to a departed friend:

CONRAD

On and on
My love for you
Goes on and on
Never dying
No Good-Byeing
Fear lost its grip
As my mind slips
Into another paradigm
Classified only by light
Another friend in flight
Flying high into the stars
While beads of color trapped in jars
Kill the pain and remain
A constant change of
Pace to replace
Another friend lost in grace

Believe these words
They are the way
I only can express
No way to say
If my wasted mind
Could re-instate itself
No matter no wealth
I only want your kind

There she is walking through the sun
In transparent majesty. Life just begun
The eyes of an eagle with a tint of the sky
Infinite love for this creature of light
A friend of the Dragonfly dimensions regroup
A teacher of life has now cut the loop
Gifted with powers of Shamanic extent
Revealing the need for more love to lament

© 1966 Bennett E. Poinsett[11] (**Betsie966@aol.com**)

Afterword

Thank you so much to all of you who have supported our work, attended our seminars, contacted us, and given us encouragement. We honor your lives and present this work in honor of the multitudes of children on Earth who are in a position to change humanity.

We love them all!

— **Lee Carroll** and **Jan Tober**

Endnotes

1. *The Columbia Dictionary of Quotations* is licensed from Columbia University Press. Copyright © 1993, 1995, by Columbia University Press. All rights reserved.

2. *Children of the New Millennium: Children's Near-Death Experiences and the Evolution of Humankind*; P.M.H. Atwater; Three Rivers Press; September 1999; ISBN 0609803093.

3. *Old Souls: The Scientific Evidence of Past Lives*; Tom Shroder; Simon & Schuster; 1999; ISBN 068485192X.

4. *Golden Rules: The Ten Ethical Values Parents Need to Teach Their Children;* Wayne Dosick; Harper; August 1998; ISBN 0061013285.

5. *Understanding Your Life Through Color;* Nancy Tappe; 1982; Starling Publishers; ISBN 0-940399-008. This book is not widely distributed. To obtain, call Awakenings Book Store in California (947) 457-0797; or Mind, Body, Soul Bookstore in Indiana (317) 889-3612.

6. *Healing the Child Within: Discovery and Recovery for Adult Children of Dysfunctional Families*; Charles L. Whitfield; Heath Communications; January 1989; ISBN: 0932194400.

7. *Recovery of Your Inner Child;* Lucia Capacchione; Fireside; March 1991; ISBN 0671701355.

8. *The Power of Your Other Hand: A Course in Channeling the Inner Wisdom of the Right Brain;* Lucia Capacchione; Newcastle Publishing Co; August 1988; ISBN 0878771301.

9. *The Care and Feeding of Indigo Children;* Doreen Virtue, Ph.D.; Hay House; August 2001; ISBN 1561708461.

10. *Can Students End School Violence?: Solutions from America's Youth;* Jason Ryan Dorsey; November 1999; JayMar Services; ISBN 1929749007.

11. From *The Dragonfly Collection: Poems and Songs by Bennett E. Poinsett;* Publisher: Shakti-Hill House.

About the Authors

Lee Carroll

After graduating with a business and economics degree from California Western University in California, Lee Carroll started a technical audio business in San Diego that flourished for 30 years. As an engineer, where do channelling and Indigo children fit into all this? As Lee tells it, God had to hit him "between the eyes" to prove his spiritual experience was real. The year 1989 was the turning point when the first psychic told him about his spiritual path, and then three years later when the second unrelated psychic told him the same thing!

Timidly, the first writings were presented to the metaphysical community in Del Mar, California, and the rest is history—a total of nine metaphysical books were released in a seven-year span. There are now over a half a million books in print in 15 languages: Spanish, French, German, Chinese, Hebrew, English, Danish, Italian, Greek, Hungarian, Japanese, Finish, Russian, Dutch, and Turkish.

Lee and his spiritual partner, Jan Tober, started the "Kryon light groups" in Del Mar in 1991 and quickly moved from a living-room setting to a Del Mar church. Now they're hosting meetings all over the globe, with audiences of up to 3,000 people in Europe alone. In the beginning days of the

Internet, Kryon had the largest consistent New Age folder in the history of America Online, and now attracts many more electronic browsers on his Website, which you can visit at **www.kryon.com**. Also on the Website is an on-line magazine where new Kryon and Indigo-related articles are featured regularly.

Perhaps the most moving meeting with Jan and Lee occurred in Tel Aviv, Israel, in October 2000. Amid the strife and violent uprisings at that time in the Middle East, messages were given to a single group of more than 1,000 Israelites that were uplifting and positive. (This message is available on the Kryon Website, listed above.)

In 1995, Lee and Jan were asked to present the Kryon work at the United Nations (U.N.) in New York City before a U.N.-chartered group known as the Society for Enlightenment and Transformation (S.E.A.T.). The meeting was so well accepted that they were invited back two more times, in 1996 and in 1998, to present their message of love!

Lee is the author of nine Kryon books, and is the co-author (along with Jan) of *The Indigo Children: The New Kids Have Arrived.* The Indigo Child Website is: **www.indigochild.com**.

Lee continues to write from his home in San Diego, living with his wife, Patricia, and his Maltese dog, Mini.

Lee Carroll (*e-mail:* **kryonemail@kryon.com**)

Jan Tober

Jan Tober has been an active metaphysician all her life. Over the past 25 years, she has worked as an intuitive counselor, hands-on healer, channel, meditation facilitator/leader, Reiki Master, co-founder of the Church of Awareness (San Diego, California), and co-facilitator of the Kryon workshops and seminars throughout the world.

Starting in her late teens, Jan's voice was her primary healing tool. At 18 years of age, she was hired to work with the jazz great, Stan Kenton, and went on to sing, record, and tour with two other legends: Benny Goodman and Fred Astaire. These men were her mentors as well as her teachers.

As part of her ongoing commitment to her spiritual work, Jan has presented three times for the Society for Enlightenment (S.E.A.T.) at the United Nations in New York City, along with Lee. Jan is the featured singer/composer on several channelled meditation albums. She has also recently released "Teknicolour Tapestry," a musical album accompanied by harpist Mark Geisler and bestselling Canadian artist Robert Coxon. This album features channelled music for healing, including the much-requested toning of voices and Tibetan singing bowls.

Jan Tober (*e-mail:* **kryonemail@kryon.com**)

We hope you enjoyed this Hay House book.
If you would like to receive a free catalog
featuring additional Hay House books and products,
or if you would like information about the
Hay Foundation, please contact:

Hay House, Inc.
P.O. Box 5100
Carlsbad, CA 92018-5100

(760) 431-7695 or **(800) 654-5126**
(760) 431-6948 (fax) or **(800) 650-5115 (fax)**

Please visit the Hay House Website at:
www.hayhouse.com